# DRESSMAKING

*A*
*Step-by-Step*
*Course*

# DRESSMAKING

## A
## *Step-by-Step*
## *Course*

## LEILA AITKEN

Sterling Publishing Co., Inc. New York

# Acknowledgements

The author and publishers would like to
thank Pat Beaumont of Style Patterns and
New Home Sewing Machines for their
help and support in the publishing of this book.

**Library of Congress Cataloging-in-Publication Data**

Aitken, Leila.
    [Step-by-step dressmaking course]
    Dressmaking : a step-by-step course / Leila Aitken.
        p.    cm.
    Originally published in Great Britain in 1992 under title: Step-by-
step dressmaking course.
    Includes index.
    ISBN 0-8069-0627-8
    1. Dressmaking.    2. Tailoring (Women's)    3. Serging.    I. Title.
TT515.A36    1994
646.4'04—dc20                                    93–43378
                                                 CIP

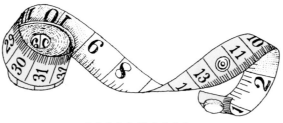

1 3 5 7 9 10 8 6 4 2

Published 1994 by Sterling Publishing Company, Inc.
387 Park Avenue South, New York, N.Y. 10016
Originally published in Great Britain by BBC Books
a division of BBC Enterprises Limited
under the title *Step-by-Step Dressmaking Course*
© 1992 by Leila Aitken, diagrams © by Kate Simunek,
photographs © 1992 by Style Patterns
Distributed in Canada by Sterling Publishing
% Canadian Manda Group, P.O. Box 920, Station U
Toronto, Ontario, Canada M8Z 5P9
*Printed and bound in Hong Kong*

Sterling ISBN 0-8069-0627-8

# CONTENTS

# INTRODUCTION

It was just over 21 years ago that two friends asked me to show them how to make a skirt. Skirts in those days and in the seaside town where I live were thick, pleated and tweedy – indispensable, though not exactly a fashion item! We chose a fairly simple pattern, some pure new wool fabric and, with one sewing machine between us, decided on a specific day to meet each week.

After six weeks they had made exactly what they wanted – skirts that fitted, in the fabric they had chosen and in the colours they preferred – soft, muted colours (at a time when most skirts seemed to be navy blue or brown!). Another friend then asked to join them and the idea of setting up a sewing school with small morning classes for adults was born.

Now, 21 years later, it is even more satisfying to teach people to sew, mainly because, over the years, we made every mistake it is possible to make and learned a great deal from them. Teaching is largely a matter of anticipating trouble and taking avoiding action. For example, things like making two left sleeves or putting the right sleeve in the left armhole don't happen any more (well, not often) because we have a sewing routine to follow that guards against it. Zips go in first time and, when following a step-by-step method carefully, they are not a problem.

And that is what this book is about. It is a step-by-step book of dressmaking based on the classes given over the last 21 years and the lessons learned both by me and all those I have taught.

I should like *you* to feel that this is a correspondence course in dressmaking. Follow each step carefully – don't take short cuts – you will find it takes longer to unpick mistakes than it does to follow the correct procedure in the first place. I know!

Dressmaking is both a rewarding hobby and a way of saving a great deal of money. It is therapeutic and satisfying – who minds a wet day when you are cosily sewing with the radio or music in the background?

The more you sew the more you will learn. You will make very successful clothes and you will also make some that you are a little disappointed with. So learn from them. Why are you not as pleased this time? Is it the fabric? Would the style have been better in a plain colour? Or would a combination of textures of fabric, a satin bodice with a velvet skirt, for example, have given a more professional-looking result? Or would a combination of a patterned and a plain fabric have worked better? Making something which you are not entirely delighted with will not prevent you from wearing it, but it will make you choose more carefully next time.

There are some very exciting fabrics on the market and you will be able to buy good quality fabric to sew with. You can make a jacket in a double jersey wool for about a third of the cost of a similar made-up garment. There will be no more wandering around shops for hours only to find that the dress you want is not available in your size – unless you take it in bottle green when you had really fancied a soft pink. Like my pupils, you can choose the colour you want in a style you like (and which suits you!) in a pattern which is designed for your size and figure-type.

# TOOLS OF THE TRADE

▶ *What you will need*

▶ *Tailoring equipment*

▶ *The sewing machine*

If you were taking up painting, sculpture or pottery, you would go out and buy all the tools you needed to practise those crafts. So why is it that dressmakers struggle on with whatever tools they have and feel guilty at spending money on their craft? Is it because we feel we have to save money when we sew?

Forget it! If you're saving money on clothes, you can spend it on the equipment you need. After all, one day you are going to take a length of pure silk or fine wool challis and stitch it into a beautifully flowing and flattering dress. That is art! And to get to that stage there are quite a few tools which will be of considerable help, not to mention necessity.

The other thing you *do* need to make dressmaking easier and more enjoyable, is space.

Ideally you should have your own small sewing room where you can leave out all your tools and, in particular, your sewing machine, ready for use. In any spare minute you can then carry on again with your sewing, leaving it when you are interrupted. However, if this is not possible, using part of a spare room or even a large desk which can be given over exclusively to your sewing, is the next best thing. If space cannot be made, try to give over half or even whole days or evenings to your hobby, to make getting the tools out worthwhile.

Whatever you do – make time! Steal it from things that are far less fun like the ironing or the housework – but I shall leave that to you!

# WHAT YOU WILL NEED

## ▶ MEASURING TAPE

A flexible tape with both metric and inch markings is useful. Metal-tipped ends give it a longer life.

## ▶ GLASS-HEADED PINS

These are sharper than ordinary pins, easier to handle and are not as easily lost.

## ▶ SCISSORS

You will need two pairs of good quality scissors to begin with – general purpose dressmaker's scissors, and a small pair of scissors about 12 cm (5 in) for clipping and trimming inside-seam turnings. Eventually you will also want to buy a pair of long-bladed dressmaker's shears for cutting out.

Good scissors should last a lifetime if they are kept only for dressmaking and never used to cut anything else – especially *not* cardboard.

## ▶ NEEDLES AND THIMBLE

The smaller the needle you use, the better the hand sewing you will achieve. Buy a packet of assorted needles and a thimble.

## ▶ STEAM IRON

For perfect dressmaking, whatever you sew, you press. Sleeve heads are the only exception (see p. 44). So a really good steam iron with extra bursts of steam is a must. Keep any old sheets, linen drying-cloths and muslin squares handy as pressing cloths.

## ▶ TAILOR'S CHALK

Essential for marking – even something as simple as the wrong side of a fabric when this is not obvious. It's available in different colours, in pencils or blocks. The blocks should be kept sharpened to a fine edge.

## ▶IRONING BOARD

A very large ironing board is a boon for pressing pleats and hems, and a metallic heat-reflecting cover is ideal.

## ▶MEASUREMENT GAUGE

There are several types of inexpensive gauges on the market. They are indispensable for using to measure the 1.5 cm ($\frac{5}{8}$ in) seam allowance as you tack.

## ▶SKIRT-HEM MARKER

There are two types:
1   The most accurate is a wooden ruler on a stand – which needs a second pair of hands.
2   A skirt marker with a bulb, which puffs powdered chalk at the hemline, means you can measure a hemline single-handed.

## ▶QUICK UNPICK

Not essential. Use with caution as a seam ripper. Useful for cutting buttonholes.

## ▶DRESSMAKER'S DUMMY

Not essential except for when adding a lining to a jacket.

# TAILORING EQUIPMENT

When you progress to tailoring a jacket you will also need:

## ▶POUNDING BLOCK

This is just a block of wood which can be easily improvised. It is used with the steam iron to pound the steam into a collar and jacket front edge. Also useful for setting pleats.

## ▶TAILOR'S HAM

This is a ham-shaped pillow for pressing curves and contours. Make one by joining two ham-shaped pieces of fabric together, leaving an opening. Stuff it very firmly with polyester toy-filling until it is hard and smooth. Oversew the opening together. See fig. 130 on p. 97.

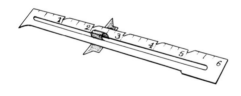

# THE SEWING MACHINE

This is the biggest help of all. It is a mistake to think that you will make do with your neighbour's hand machine until you see if you get keen on dressmaking. A good sewing machine is a joy to use and will turn you into an enthusiastic home sewer. An erratic sewing machine is a labour and a chore and will effectively dampen all the enthusiasm you have when you first start dressmaking.

Computerised sewing machines are wonderful, not least because they are so easy to use. You see the picture of the stitch you need and you press the visual-display screen. These machines give even stitching on many thicknesses of fabric and bulky corners, do superb and effortless buttonholes, and an amazing variety of decorative stitches and letters for personal monograms.

The computerised sewing machine is the Rolls-Royce of sewing machines and every beginner should have one! However, every beginner may not be able to afford one and if this is the case there are many machines at the other end of the price scale which a beginner may feel more confident about choosing and are almost as good an investment.

Equally, a very basic sewing machine is not a very good investment. It will not do as much to help you and you will very soon demand more of your machine.

What you need is a machine that will constantly give you a good, balanced stitch (fiddling with tension discs is just a memory these days). After that basic priority, you can choose from:

● free-arm machines which have a zigzag stitch and a buttonholer, which is a bit of a labour. These are not very exciting.

● middle range machines which have a stretch stitch facility, and therefore a wider range of utility and decorative stitches, with an automatic buttonhole facility (which is much easier to use).

● electronic machines (not to be confused with computerised machines) with electronic needle penetration and foot control, giving superb stitching and LED indication of the pattern selected, much better buttonholes and other exciting possibilities.

It is confusing for a beginner to choose a sewing machine without help. Do try to buy the best you can possibly afford – it will pay for itself in the end. You will get a great deal of pleasure from a machine that purrs along efficiently and gives perfect results; and nothing but frustration from a machine that wastes valuable time getting snarled up and which is no encouragement to you at all.

Overlock machines have added another dimension to dressmaking, and overlocking is dealt with in a separate section in this book (see p. 105). They are the home version of the industrial machine. Overlocking gives a professional finish to seams and edges by cutting and finishing the seam in one operation. They also sew extremely quickly. As you progress with dressmaking you will almost certainly want an overlocker. This does not replace your ordinary machine but is used in conjunction with it. It is worth considering when you buy a sewing machine whether you want to buy a 'combi' – which is a combination of the overlocker and an ordinary machine.

Whichever machine you choose, check on the after-sales care and servicing available in your area.

## CHAPTER ONE

# CHOOSING YOUR PATTERN

▸ *Designer ease and multi-sized patterns*

▸ *How to measure yourself*

▸ *Know your figure*

There has never been a better or a more exciting time to learn how to sew: developments in fabric technology mean that there are easier fabrics to work with, patterns are multi-sized which minimises the fitting problem, and the arrival of the overlock sewing machine on the domestic market brings a couture finish to hand-made clothes.

But before you can start on your sewing course you need to decide what you are going to make and if there is a special fabric you just cannot resist. Getting the right style for you is a skill you will develop with practice. To help make the right decision with your first pattern I suggest you buy a large pattern catalogue, one that has just recently been discontinued. Any fabric shop will sell it to you at a token cost.

Pattern catalogues, from which you choose your designs, are issued to fabric shops and departments several times a year and with each issue new designs are added and others discarded. Spend some time browsing through the catalogue to familiarise yourself with the layout, the sizings and the design features of the clothes in each of the different sections.

The photographs in the catalogue are, of course, an inspiration. You must ask yourself if *you* are going to look like the models in the pictures. Several different garments and styles will probably appeal to you when you first see them. 'I'd love to make that' you might think, but then another thought may occur, 'Will it suit *me*?'.

The clothes in the catalogue are modelled by men and women who have apparently perfect figures – something which the rest of us may not have. Most of us camouflage our 'bad' points carefully – we know that some styles flatter us more than others and a little discrimination in our choice of pattern will make all the difference.

The two words 'line' and 'silhouette' crop up often in pattern design. The elusive quality of line is the sense of design that flows through the body from top-to-toe, to complete the total look of a garment or outfit. The aim in dressmaking is to achieve a graceful, flattering, unbroken and harmonious line.

The silhouette, on the other hand, is the outline shape of the garment on the actual person and the aim here is to choose the shape which works best for an individual's figure. For example, a shape or silhouette that is broader at the top than at the bottom, such as a batwing sleeved dress with a straight skirt, can be flattering to a person with a small bust, because it gives weight at the top of the body. However, a fitted bodice with a full flowing skirt gives weight at the bottom of the body, thereby making a waistline look smaller than it actually is.

The construction lines on a garment can also be used to create illusions. Emphasised vertical lines, such as front openings, princess-line seams (these are the seams which form long, unbroken panels in a dress which has no waist-line seam), and elongated pleat lines are all slimming. The same effect can be achieved by using striped fabric, asymmetric lines and checks cut on the bias. Diagonal lines across the body are also slimming. A cross-over bodice or a V-neck has the same slimming effect as a vertical line.

On the other hand, the opposite to this – that stripes used horizontally are fattening – is not absolutely true; it depends on the stripe. A very narrow stripe used horizontally can still give a slimming effect. However, horizontal lines which break up the silhouette, such as those on a box jacket, or waist and yoke seams, will cut the height and these do add to the width of the body. The lower the line cuts the silhouette, the shorter and therefore the wider the figure will appear.

A heavy figure will also appear larger in a very fitted dress made up in a stiff fabric – such as a cotton shirtwaister. A dress in a softer fabric, say a cotton jersey, will be an easier fit and will give a little fullness to drape gracefully over the body in gentle folds, making it much more slimming.

In the same way, dresses with bodices that are gently bloused over the waistline are more slimming than a fitted corseted look. A wide belt, 5 cm (2 in) or more, is surprisingly much more slimming than a narrow belt; and a curved belt, worn low at the front, is best of all.

This is all advice for the not so slim; but very thin people also have their own problems. However, they are easier to deal with because it is easy to create the illusion of bulk with textured fabrics, horizontal lines which break the silhouette, high necklines, and all the things larger-figured people are doing their best to avoid. Colour can also add bulk or seem to reduce an outline – see Choosing your Fabric on page 21.

Before you make the final decision about which pattern to buy, go and look at fabrics (see chapter 2). Combining pattern and fabric is a very important part of successful dressmaking which needs care and imagination! If you cannot make up your mind which pattern to choose you may find that the fabric will be the deciding factor.

The cost, washability and design of any fabric should be taken into consideration in relation to the pattern you want to buy. Read this chapter before you rush out to buy your pattern.

# DESIGNER EASE

Patterns are always slightly larger than your actual body measurements – even fitted styles – because they need to allow you room to move in your clothes. This is known as 'ease'. The basic ease allowed on a pattern does not vary very much. It is approximately 6.5 cm ($2\frac{1}{2}$ in) on the bust; 2.5 cm (1 in) on the waist and 5 cm (2 in) on the hips. There is less on patterns designed for knit fabrics.

Fashion, however, often dictates the use of a great deal more room than the basic ease, e.g. to give a wide silhouette or loose-flowing lines. This is known as designer ease. It varies greatly from one designer to another. It is a mistake to try and alter the amount of designer ease or to take a smaller pattern than your correct size, as this will destroy the look the designer intended and therefore the look for which you chose the pattern. It is also a mistake to keep your patterns for too long because, without your realising it, the cut of your pattern can be very out of date. For example, armhole shapes have altered drastically over the last few years, as have trouser patterns, which are now cut with a fairly flat front with most of the shaping on the back trouser piece.

# MULTI-SIZED PATTERNS

Multi-sized patterns are a fairly recent introduction and they are a boon. As the name implies, many pattern sizes are printed on the one pattern tissue, with the cutting line for each size clearly indicated. This means that extensive pattern alteration is a thing of the past. If, for example, you are a size 14 bust but have size 16 hips, you do not need to alter your pattern; you simply transfer smoothly from the size 14 cutting line to the size 16 cutting line as you move from the hip to the waist when you cut the pattern out.

But because of the number of cutting lines on the pattern, a beginner may find this confusing. When you have identified the line indicating your own size, cut out the pattern on that line right away before you lay it out on the fabric. Alternatively, if you want to cut out pattern and fabric together and do not want to cut out twice, draw over the line you need with a brightly coloured text marker.

# TAKING YOUR MEASUREMENTS

For the home dressmaker, a large number of complicated body measurements is unnecessary: you will still obtain a good fit from your pattern by taking a few essential measurements very carefully. There are two lists of

**1** Measure bust, waist and hips around the fullest part

measurements you will need: first, there are measurements from which you determine your size and figure type (this is the name given to your figure-type by pattern designers, i.e. Misses' or Women's), and secondly, a further list, to which you will refer later, to adjust your pattern where necessary.

First, fill in your body measurements and then refer to the sizing chart to determine which type and pattern size correspond most closely to your own measurements. (If you have a very full bust, with a difference of 5 cm (2 in) or more between bust and high bust measurements, then you will find the high bust measurement more accurate in determining your nearest pattern size.) See Your Personal Measurement Chart opposite. An abbreviated version of the Standard Pattern-sizing Chart is included opposite. A comprehensive chart, including men and children's sizes, as well as figure-types, is given at the back of pattern catalogues.

Now fill in the second list of measurements, this time for the garment, so that you have all the measurements you will need for making up your outfit. Lengths are given on the back of the pattern envelope and, where these are appropriate, check with the chart and not the tissue pattern itself.

Even if you feel you already know your size, fill in the chart just to make quite sure that you choose the best pattern for your figure. Take your measurements while wearing only your underwear and a petticoat (if you wear one). Get someone to help you if you can. Take the measurements accurately, snugly but not tightly, and record them on the chart opposite. Tie a length of soft, narrow elastic around your waist to mark your waistline before you start (see Figs 2 and 4).

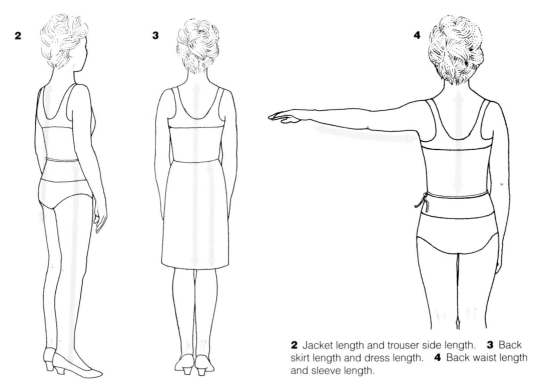

**2** Jacket length and trouser side length. **3** Back skirt length and dress length. **4** Back waist length and sleeve length.

## YOUR PERSONAL MEASUREMENT CHART

### Body Measurements

| NAME<br>DATE | MINE | PATTERN | ADJUSTMENTS | |
|---|---|---|---|---|
| | | | PLUS | MINUS |
| **HEIGHT** | | | | |
| **BUST (around fullest part, straight across the back, under the arms)** | | | | |
| **HIGH BUST (across the widest part of the back, high under the arms)** | | | | |
| **WAIST (around natural waistline)** | | | | |
| **HIPS (around fullest part)** | | | | |

**MY PATTERN SIZE IS** _____

### Standard Pattern-sizing Chart

Measurement Chart

| Size | 6 | 8 | 10 | 12 | 14 | 16 | 18 | |
|---|---|---|---|---|---|---|---|---|
| **Bust** | 78 | 80 | 83 | 87 | 92 | 97 | 102 | cms |
| | $30\frac{1}{2}$ | $31\frac{1}{2}$ | $32\frac{1}{2}$ | 34 | 36 | 38 | 40 | inches |
| **Waist** | 58 | 61 | 64 | 67 | 71 | 76 | 81 | cms |
| | 23 | 24 | 25 | $26\frac{1}{2}$ | 28 | 30 | 32 | inches |
| **Hip** | 83 | 85 | 88 | 92 | 97 | 102 | 107 | cms |
| | $32\frac{1}{2}$ | $33\frac{1}{2}$ | $34\frac{1}{2}$ | 36 | 38 | 40 | 42 | inches |

*Pattern Measurements*

| NAME _____ DATE _____ | MINE | PATTERN | ADJUSTMENTS PLUS | MINUS |
|---|---|---|---|---|
| **BACK WAIST LENGTH (from nape of neck to waist)** | | | | |
| **BACK SKIRT LENGTH (from back waist to desired length of skirt)** | | | | |
| **DRESS LENGTH (from nape of neck to desired length)** | | | | |
| **TROUSER SIDE LENGTH (from waist to below ankle bone)** | | | | |
| **JACKET LENGTH (from nape of neck to desired length)** | | | | |
| **SLEEVE LENGTH (from underarm to wrist, with the arm straight) Average arm is 46 cm (18 ins).** | | | | |

# KNOW YOUR FIGURE

There is no such thing as the perfect figure. After all, in some countries the slender woman is an object of pity! But most of us have some idea of the way we'd like to look and it's usually not exactly the way we are!

Making your own clothes means that you can make the most of your figure by camouflaging what you consider to be your bad points and emphasising your good ones.

The following guide has been designed to help you identify your figure-type and to help you look for the best design features in different garments. Of course, there are lots of variations of these 'types' of figure – look out for the design features that may be useful for *your* figure.

A

▶ **A** TALL AND SLENDER

● **AVOID**
● Unbelted princess lines
● Lots of monotonous plain colour
● Sharply tailored angular lines

● **CHOOSE**
● Double breasted jackets with softly tailored raglan shoulders
● Belted dresses with gathers or pleats from the shoulders
● Contrasting colours for separates, include patterned fabric to relieve the plain
● Pants with fullness at the waist, or hip detail and cuffs

▶ **A** SHORT AND SLENDER

● **AVOID**
● Sharp contrasts in separates
● Double breasted jackets in large checks
● Large floral designs, horizontal lines, long length jackets

● **CHOOSE**
● Colour co-ordinated separates
● Narrow-legged pants with loose-fitting tops, waist length jackets
● Shoulder and neck details, such as stand up collars, shoulder yokes, epaulettes, narrow lapels

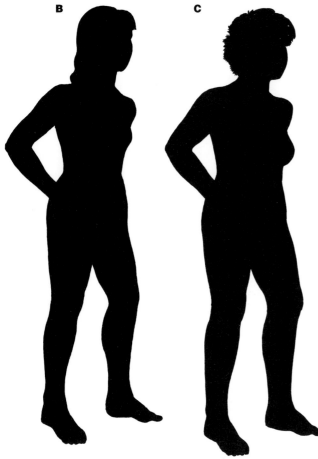

B    C

### ▶ B SHORT AND HEAVY

- **AVOID**
- Contrasts in colour with separates
- Horizontal seam lines, narrow belts, very short skirts
- Large checks, dominant pattern

- **CHOOSE**
- Blouson tops finishing at the top of the hip to elongate the body
- Vertical seam lines, V necks, rever collars
- Longline cardigan-style jackets
- Co-ordinating colour schemes

### ▶ C TOP HEAVY

- **AVOID**
- Fitted bodices
- Large patterns and bright and shiny fabric above the waist
- Shoulder yokes, horizontal seam lines, boxy jackets

- **CHOOSE**
- Easy fitting dresses with softly gathered shoulders in fabrics which drape well
- Long-line jackets, loosely fitting with centred buttons and vertical seam lines
- Pants, skirts and culottes with hip detail, waist tucks and pockets, straight legged pants with tunic tops

### ▶ B TALL AND HEAVY

- **AVOID**
- A tight fit
- Unnecessary detail and clutter
- A large expanse of plain or shiny fabric and brash colours

- **CHOOSE**
- Toning shades of mid to dark colours, accents of strong colour can be added with accessories
- Judicious use of patterned fabric
- Softly tailored single-breasted jackets, flared skirts
- loosely fitting clothes that skim the figure to give a kinder silhouette

### ▶ C BOTTOM HEAVY

- **AVOID**
- Hip pockets, skirts on a basque, detail below the waist
- Shorts, tight straight skirts, culottes
- Waist length jackets

- **CHOOSE**
- Blouses with neck collar and shoulder detail
- Easy fitting long jackets, with tailored shoulders and pads
- Bright colours and pattern for above and dark plain colours for below the waist

## CHAPTER TWO

# CHOOSING YOUR FABRIC

> *Learn how to select the best fabric for your garment*

> *Learn about natural and man-made fabrics*

> *Learn about woven, knit and luxury fabrics*

Choosing your fabric is just as exciting as choosing your pattern and requires the same amount of careful thought and planning. Before you buy your fabric, look at the information on the back of the pattern envelope. There, as well as the chart showing the amount of fabric you will need in the correct fabric width, you will find a list of the different types of fabrics suitable for making up the pattern you have bought. Follow these suggestions because they have been made by the designer and you obviously want to achieve as close a copy of the original illustration of the garment as you can. The many different fabrics suggested by the designer will all give slightly varied looks to the pattern. You need to think about the look you want to achieve. Above all, buy something which is good quality.

The colour of the fabric is the next most significant influence on the finished look of the pattern. The delightful thing about dressmaking is that you can make colour work for you and really enjoy using it.

Colour can affect mood. Some colours are really pleasing to look at. Usually warm colours, like yellow and pink, can make you feel at ease and relaxed; cool colours, like blue and turquoise, can stimulate and challenge; cold colours, like slate grey and purple, can make you feel distant and dignified!

Colours worn near the face can enhance the skin tones or clash violently with them. As a general guide, those colours which complement the eyes are flattering. Colour also affects the body in silhouette. Dark colours such as navy and black give a slimmer outline because they 'recede', whereas a bright shade of pink or red will 'advance' and make the figure more defined.

Try colours near your face, as it is important to discover those colours which suit you. Also, unroll a length of a fabric you like and hold it up in front of a mirror so you can see how it looks in a larger piece. You will also be able to see how it moves if you do this. But remember that it is clever colour co-ordination that makes a really successful outfit. Look at the colours which have been teamed together in the pattern catalogue as well as the displays in the fabric shops. Some of the most eye-catching outfits use new and original colour combinations – orange with pale pink is one example! Don't be influenced by 'fashion' colours. If they don't suit you, ignore them!

Look out for fabrics sold in the shop as 'mix and match' co-ordinates, such as checks with toning plain fabrics, or florals teamed with a spotted fabric in matching colours. The colours have been chosen by a fabric designer and make up into professional-looking outfits.

Fabric texture also adds interest to garments and, just as using only one colour can be monotonous, so too can making up an outfit that is all-shiny or has an all-over pattern. People are understandably a little wary of using fabric with very large designs, but in fact a small all-over design, unrelieved by a break in colour, can also be difficult to use and wear.

As a general rule, distinctive patterns are best 'anchored' by teaming with plain fabrics. And if you want to keep to one all-over plain colour then use contrasts in texture – a fluffy mohair with a smooth worsted wool, for example, or a matt fabric with a shiny one.

Although the best way to learn about fabric is to use it, it is helpful to know something about how it is made.

All fabric is made from yarn. Yarns are the threads used in weaving the cloth. These yarns can be made from natural fibres, obtained from animals and vegetables, or the yarn can be man-made from fibres which are constructed chemically.

These two groups of fibres can be combined either when the fibre is spun into yarn, or when the yarns are woven into cloth. Combining these two groups by blending or mixing the fibres in this way has definite advantages. It can make the yarn stronger or, sometimes, cheaper and it allows variation of weight, producing an infinite variety of yarns and fabric.

# NATURAL FIBRES

These are cotton, linen, wool and silk.

## ▶ COTTON

Cotton is the most widely used textile fibre. It is produced from cotton, a fibrous substance which grows on a shrub in countries where there is plenty of rain and sunshine. Egypt and India are cotton-producing countries, but the finest cotton is Egyptian cotton. Fabric which is made from cotton is strong, absorbent, comfortable to wear and washes well, although it also creases easily. When it is treated with chemicals a smoother cotton is produced with a high lustre and better dye uptake, and is known as mercerised cotton.

## ▶ LINEN

Linen is less widely used in home dressmaking than it used to be, partly because it is expensive. It is made from the inner fibres of the flax plant. Fabrics made from linen are even stronger than cotton; they are cool to wear and very absorbent. Linen creases rather badly, but it has advantages when it is mixed with other yarns and is hard-wearing and often used for home furnishings.

## ▶ WOOL

Wool is many people's favourite fabric and comes from sheep. Different breeds of sheep produce very different wools. Cross-bred sheep produce a tough, hard-wearing wool. A high proportion of the wool used in home dressmaking comes from the Merino sheep from Australia and South Africa which produce a fine, superb quality fleece. Mohair and cashmere both come from the hair of goats and angora comes from rabbits. Alpaca, vicuña and llama all come from the hair of animals of the same name. The quality of wool depends on the length (or staple length, as it is called) and diameter of the fibre. The finer the diameter the higher the quality. The term 'worsted' is used for wool made from the longest fibres. It is made into a smooth round yarn of parallel fibres from a high-quality fleece. Pure wool is a very warm and comfortable fabric to wear, but it is not a strong fibre when used on its own. It sheds creases and drapes well.

## ▶ SILK

Silk is made from the cocoon of the silk moth. The silk caterpillar does most of the work, spinning fibres into a cocoon which is unravelled and used to make the thread which is known as a filament. The main producers of silk are now in the Far East. Silk is warm to the touch, delightful to wear, and is elastic and lustrous. Tussah silk is produced from the cocoons spun by wild silkworms; it is thicker and has less sheen than the filament of the cultivated silkworm. Spun silk is made from shorter filaments of waste silk or defective cocoons.

# MAN-MADE FIBRES

Man-made fibres are manufactured by the chemical treatment of certain raw materials such as wood-pulp and oil. Although the term man-made applies to all fibres not naturally produced, there are two types: synthetic fibres, which are those made completely from oil, and regenerated fibres made from cellulose, usually made from wood-pulp which is a natural product. The main features of all man-made fibres are their strength and plasticity. New developments in these fibres regularly appear on the market under various trade names, but they can be grouped under generic headings. Some names you will come across in dressmaking are polyester, acrylic, acetate, viscose, nylon and spandex.

### ▶ POLYESTER

A fibre of exceptional strength, widely used in combination with natural fibres to give durability. It is crease resistant, but will retain heat-set creases and pleats and it needs little or no ironing. It crops up in many forms, nowadays it is often difficult to distinguish from the real thing. E.g. polyester silk, polyester jersey etc.

### ▶ ACRYLIC

This is a soft, bulky and wool-like fibre, warm to handle and hard wearing. It does not crease readily and keeps its shape although it tends to cling. E.g. knitwear and fleece fabrics.

### ▶ ACETATE

This makes a cheap, but attractive, silky fabric which is usually shiny. It creases readily and is not strong. E.g. taffeta and lining fabrics.

### ▶ VISCOSE

This is now unrecognisable as its former cheap and shiny image. Spun viscose can have all the draping qualities and soft handle of fine wool. It is dyed in glowing colours and is crease resistant.

### ▶ NYLON

This is a very strong, lightweight fibre which is elastic and does not crease. It is also warm and quick drying. Its disadvantage is that it clings and holds the body heat, therefore making the skin clammy. E.g. tricot.

### ▶ SPANDEX

A strong fibre with a lot of stretch. It is lightweight and quick drying, and its tradename is widely known as Lycra.

# WOVEN FABRICS

Woven fabrics are made by interweaving vertical and horizontal threads. The lengthwise threads are known as the warp and the widthwise threads as the weft. Extra threads, sometimes stronger or of a different colour, can be placed in the warp at each end to give the fabric a good edge which is known as the selvedge.

Satin is woven by missing out warp threads and allowing the weft to float over several

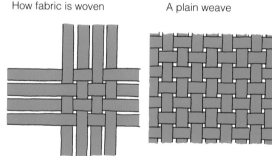

How fabric is woven

A plain weave

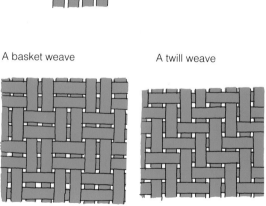

A basket weave

A twill weave

threads at one time, which gives the fabric its characteristic shine.

Loom attachments and special looms are used to produce fancy weaves such as: dobby, which is a raised geometric pattern; raised ribs such as piqué; leno, which is a very open weave used for net curtains; and Jacquard, which is a complicated patterned weave.

# KNIT FABRICS

Knit fabric is made up of a series of inter-locking loops formed from one or more yarns. The loops 'give' and open up when stretched and will return to their original shape when they are released. The term 'gauge' is used to indicate the number of stitches per quarter inch. The higher the number of stitches, the finer the knit. To judge the stretchiness of your fabric see p. 127.

Knits are made from both natural and synthetic yarns and then finished in a variety of ways to give a vast number of plain and novelty knits.

## ▶ SINGLE KNIT

A single knit, called jersey, is made in many weights – from fine, figure hugging light-weights to substantial trouser-weight jersey. A single knit has a recognisable right and wrong side, as lengthwise ribs are seen on the right side only. They also stretch more crosswise than lengthwise.

## ▶ DOUBLE KNIT

A double knit is a more stable type of weft knit. It is made by using two sets of yarns and two needles, to knit two separate layers which are interlocked. A double knit looks the same on both sides.

## ▶ RIB KNITS

Rib knits have vertical ribs on both sides of the fabric, with good crosswise stretch. Inter-lock knits are smooth-surfaced rib knits. They have good crosswise stretch and recovery.

## ▶ RASCHEL KNITS

Raschel knits are textured knits, with a tweedy, bumpy texture and an open lacy look. They need only the simplest of patterns as they have such surface interest.

## ▶ TRICOT

Tricot is a single knit with a smooth finish and excellent draping qualities. It is used for lingerie.

Knit fabrics are especially good for sport and leisure clothes. There are now many inex-pensive cotton interlock types on the market and cotton or acrylic sweatshirt knits, which are fleece-backed for comfort. Two-way stretch fabric, incorporating Lycra, is avail-able for swim-suits and cycling pants.

The amount of stretch in a knit fabric obviously varies according to the type of manufacture and also to some extent by the weight of the fabric, whether it is a light-weight or a heavy knit. For dressmaking pur-poses these are categorised as stretch knits and stable knits.

Double jersey is an example of a stable knit. It has a limited amount of stretch and is made up in the 'relaxed', i.e. unstretched, state. It is delightful to wear because the fabric yields to the shape and the movement of the body and yet returns to its original shape without creasing. Most patterns are suitable for a stable knit and conventional dressmaking as opposed to overlocking tech-niques are used. It keeps its shape well and can be tailored for style and structure.

Stretch knits, on the other hand, have a great deal of stretch and recovery. Overlocking techniques are really the only satisfactory way to make them up. (See chapters 10, 11 and 12.) A sweater knit is an example of a stretch knit.

Knit fabrics are not, however, the only stretch fabrics. A woven fabric can be constructed to accommodate a certain amount of stretch too, so that it gives with the movement of the body but will return to its original shape, e.g. stretch corduroy and denim.

# LUXURY FABRICS

## ▶ VELVET

Velvet is very rewarding, but difficult, to sew. Modern velvets are made from both natural and synthetic fibres, so that velvets vary greatly, both in quality and in price. Silk velvet is the ultimate luxury fabric, but at the other end of the scale, nylon or rayon velvet has merit for more practical clothes, as it doesn't crush and can be washed, and it wears forever. Cotton velvet is also hard-wearing and is used in furnishings.

Choose a simple pattern for velvet, with as few pieces as possible and no top-stitching or tricky design details, e.g. welt pockets. All velvet is cut using a 'with nap' layout (see p. 31). Interfacing for velvet should be sew-in, not iron-on, and pressing should be kept to a minimum.

Because velvet creeps during tacking, this may cause puckered seams. The only way to solve this problem on long seams is to pin the shoulders or waist of the garment-pieces to a padded coat hanger and suspend them from the top of a door. Then pin and tack the seams as the garment is hanging.

## ▶ SATIN

Satin is now used for all kinds of clothes, including trousers, and can be worn at any time. Use a 'with nap' layout, because the satin weave gives a shine which reflects the light in different ways. Use special wedding dress and lace pins, and as few as possible in the cutting out as some satins will mark easily. Keep tacking to a minimum and avoid taking out machine stitching! (The needle punctures the fabric and the marks often cannot be removed.)

## ▶ METALLIC FABRICS

Metallic fabrics are popular for evening wear and shiny threads, such as Lurex, are frequently woven into daytime fabrics. Cut these fabrics with old scissors (metallic fabrics will blunt your good ones) and follow a 'with nap' layout. Fabrics with a large proportion of metallic threads, which would be scratchy to wear, will need to be lined to the edge, or faced with a non-metallic fabric.

If stitching is difficult, use tissue paper under the seams as you sew (to stop the metallic threads catching). It is not possible to press most metallic fabrics with an iron, but the seams can be pressed open with the forefinger.

## ▶ LEATHER-LOOK FABRIC, SIMULATED SUEDE AND PLASTIC

These are far easier to sew than they look. Use a 'with nap' cutting layout. To hold pieces together for stitching use paper clips or staples which can be removed. Use a machine needle sold for the purpose. If light pressing is necessary use brown paper instead of a pressing cloth. Flatten seam turnings and finish hems with clear-drying adhesive.

CHAPTER THREE

# *C*UTTING OUT

*Adjusting the pattern to fit you*

*Placing the pattern*

*Cutting out*

*Marking the fabric to help with fitting the pieces together*

Before you go ahead and cut out your pattern you need to consider a few important points. First of all, do you need to make any adjustments to your pattern which will make it a better fit for you? Now is the time to do it – *before* you cut out your skirt several inches too short! Study the *back* of the pattern envelope at this stage (see p. 144). It has quite a bit of relevant information on it. For instance, the length of the garments illustrated on the front of the pattern envelope may be deceptive and so the exact finished lengths of all the garments included in the pattern are given on the back of the envelope. The lengths you need and which you noted on p. 18 should be compared with these now. (See pattern adjustment on p. 29.)

Then, have a close look at your fabric. Does it present you with any problems? Has it got a one-way design – flowers all growing in one direction, for example? Has it a pile or a sheen? Your pattern must be positioned so that any design is going the right way and the pile is lying the correct way. This chapter has lots of tips and information to help you get both of these things right before you make the first vital snip.

You should also check that your fabric is folded correctly, that it is flat when you cut it out and that you have a large surface and good scissors for the job.

To find the layout which you need to follow on the cutting out chart in the pattern, you have to know three things: first, your fabric width; secondly, the view of the pattern in the illustration that you are going to make; and finally, your pattern size. With this information you can select the cutting layout which is relevant to you. It is a good idea to circle it with a coloured pen to avoid confusion with all the other layouts.

Cutting out is one of the most important parts of dressmaking – this chapter will help you get it right!

# PATTERN ADJUSTMENT

Pattern adjustment will not make a lot of sense until you have made a few badly-fitting garments! Pattern adjustment and fitting are areas where you learn by trial and error – and more effectively by error! There are two stages in making clothes that fit: pattern adjustment and fitting.

## ▶ PATTERN ADJUSTMENT

This is checking your own list of measurements with those on the back of the pattern envelope and adjusting your paper pattern accordingly.

Multi-sized patterns mean that the only adjustments you need to make to your pattern prior to cutting out are the relevant lengths. (Refer to the pattern measurements chart on p. 17.) Check all your relevant measurements (back waist to hem length for a skirt; underarm sleeve length for a jacket or shirt; and side waist to hem length for trousers etc.) and then compare these with the lengths which

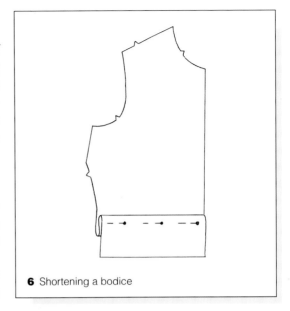

**6** Shortening a bodice

are given on the back of the pattern envelope, making a note of any necessary adjustments. It's at this stage that you should alter your pattern, referring to the following diagrams. If, for example, you need to shorten a jacket

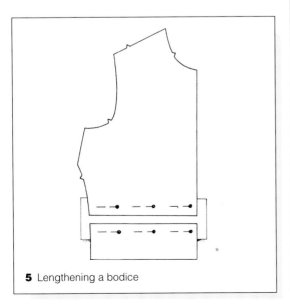

**5** Lengthening a bodice

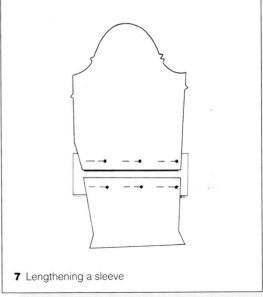

**7** Lengthening a sleeve

*29*

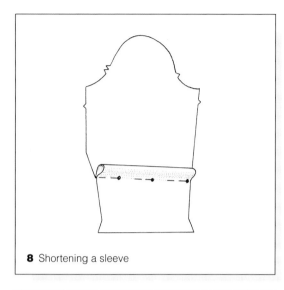

**8** Shortening a sleeve

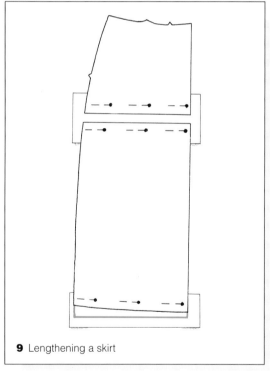

**9** Lengthening a skirt

length you will need to do this to the jacket back, front, and also the facing pieces.

The pattern will give a line to indicate where adjustments should be made to the length, but use your judgement as well. If you have a large addition to the length of a flared skirt, divide that amount between the marked line and the hemline or, in the case of a sleeve, divide it between the upper and the lower arm on all the relevant pattern pieces.

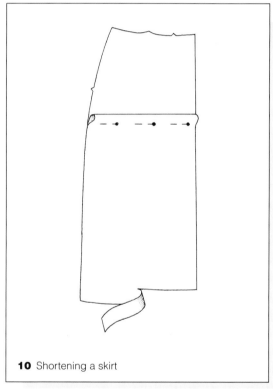

**10** Shortening a skirt

You will gradually become used to those pattern adjustments which apply specifically to you and which will apply in almost all the clothes you make. You may, for example, always need to shorten either a sleeve or a skirt.

▶FITTING

This is trying on the garment to discover the fitting problems, if any, which are peculiar to you, e.g. a hollow back, causing wrinkles in a skirt at the small of the back. Fitting is essential, because some problems will only become apparent when the pattern is made up in fabric and can only be adjusted to an individual figure at that stage.

You should also alter your pattern at this stage. This means going back to the pattern to make the same alteration to the pattern that you have already made to the fabric – so that the pattern is ready for use when you want to use it again. (See details on fitting skirts (p. 49) and trousers (p. 61) in Part Two of this book.)

## PLACING THE PATTERN

If you have chosen a plain, spotted or floral fabric which has not got any dominant or recurring pattern then you need only follow the layout instructions given on the instruction sheet. These have been thought out to help you use your fabric in the most economical way. Fold your fabric as indicated in the layout and place it on your cutting surface in the same way e.g. fold towards you and selvedges away from you.

## PLACING THE PATTERN ON DIFFICULT FABRICS

Stripes, checks, large designs and pile fabrics are all fabrics which home dressmakers often avoid. But once you understand how to deal with them, they are simply a challenge which you will enjoy. The only fabric which can be said to be really difficult is a bold diagonal stripe. With this one, take the easy way out and choose a pattern showing a diagonal

stripe in the illustration and designed specifically for that fabric, and follow the cutting layout exactly. There are also patterns designed especially for checks, stripes, borders etc., but you can use any unusual fabric for any pattern, providing the pattern does not state that it is not suitable. There may not be a cutting layout detailing exactly what you have in mind, in which case you will have to use your own judgement.

## PILE FABRICS

Velvet, corduroy and fur are the obvious pile fabrics, but suede, mohair and brushed fabric such as denim also have a pile. First determine the direction of the pile, by smoothing it with the palm of your hand. The fabric feels rough when you move your hand against the direction of the pile and smooth when it moves with it. The darkest sheen in velvet and corduroy is produced by using the fabric with the pile lying upwards. Mohair and fur are used with the pile lying downwards. Use a pattern layout marked 'with nap' – that is, with all the pattern pieces placed in the same direction. Nap layouts are indicated by asterisks on the back of the pattern envelope, so refer to these when you buy the fabric.

Fold pile fabric wrong side out when you cut or the tissue will 'creep' on the pile. Cut fur fabric through the backing only, with the point of the scissors, easing the pile apart.

## ONE-WAY DESIGNS AND SHINY FABRICS

Designs which repeat in one direction only must be cut using a 'with nap' layout. Satin, brocade, metallic fabric and most knit fabrics also use a 'with nap' layout, as the light must reflect from the surface evenly.

*31*

# STRIPES

## ▶ BALANCED STRIPES

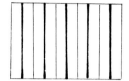

When you fold the fabric, make sure that the stripe underneath is *exactly* the same as the one on top, so that the stripes will match.

Other effects can be achieved by cutting the stripes one way on the main body pieces and the opposite way on yokes, cuffs, collars, pockets and front bands. With a horizontal stripe, cut out a skirt with the dominant stripe at the hem edge, and unless the skirt is very full, cut the hemline straight by the stripe and not curved. (To make sure which stripe is dominant look at the fabric through half-closed eyes, from a distance.) Keep the dominant line away from the fullest part of the bust. The stripes should match at all seams and at the front notch at the armhole seam.

## ▶ UNBALANCED STRIPES

An unbalanced stripe has a different arrangement of bars or colours each side of the main stripe.

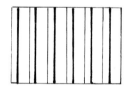

For a horizontal stripe use a cutting layout for nap fabrics. An unbalanced vertical stripe is also best cut on single fabric if you want the bars to follow the same direction around the body. (Follow the directions for uneven plaids below.)

With both types of vertical stripes, place a dominant line at the centre-front and -back of a bodice or skirt and at the sleeve head (where the sleeve is inserted into the armhole). The stripes in a two-piece outfit should line up where they overlap, e.g. jacket to skirt in a suit. Try the effect of using a single colour of stripe, or a bias cut strip, to bind crosswise edges such as pocket edges, belts or bound buttonholes, or a bias cut strip of fabric as a piping to emphasise seams.

# PLAIDS AND CHECKS

Strictly speaking a plaid is not the same thing as a check. A plaid is made up of stripes, crossing each other at right angles; a check is made up of squares like a chessboard – but in general they are both referred to as checked fabrics. Tartans, for example, are plaids.

There are two kinds of plaids: even and uneven. Isolate a square and work out, from the centre of the square. If the arrangement of bars and colours is the same in each direction, it is an even check, and presents no problem. If it is not the same in each direction it is an uneven check and can present quite a challenge.

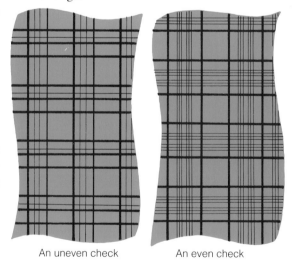

An uneven check          An even check

## ▶AN EVEN PLAID

This is not really difficult to work with. It just needs to be cut out methodically. Follow this routine when cutting out even plaids and checks:

1 Pin the fabric so that the underneath layer is exactly the same as the one on top and the fold is at the centre of a dominant line.

2 Place the front pattern with its centre-front line in the middle of the dominant check, if there is no seam, or completing a check, if there is a seam or a front opening.

3 Note the position of the lowest side seam notch on the front, below any dart, and place the back pattern piece so that the corresponding notch is on the same check, bearing in mind that it is the *seam stitching* line and not the *cutting* line you are matching.

4 Place the collar so that the collar ends finish on the same check. Try also to match the centre-back of the collar to the centre-back of the bodice, though this may not always be possible.

5 Place the sleeve with the notch in the sleeve front matching the notch in the bodice front. It is not possible to match shoulder seams or two-piece sleeve seams exactly.

6 Place the front of the skirt first, lining it up with the bodice front so that the centre line is on the same line of the plaid.

7 Place the skirt back so that the lowest notch in the side seam matches the corresponding notch in the front. If you have several skirt panels, work systematically round the skirt from front to back, matching the notches.

8 Place glass-headed pins at the side seams on the hemline, to remind you to cut a *straight* hem, along the lines of the check, and not a curve.

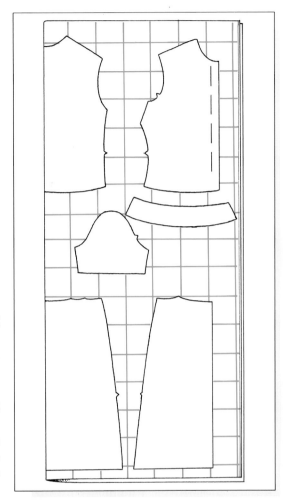

If you are short of fabric, you can reverse the pattern pieces on an even plaid to cut more economically.

Most of the facings are not very important as they do not show, but remember that front facings *will* show if the garment is worn open at the neck. Match front facings by the notches or, if you have plenty of fabric and a straight facing, you can adapt the pattern to cut the facing in one with the front. Pin the front pattern piece to the front facing, with the stitching lines matching, to give an extended facing.

You can also do away with making a seam in a plaid fabric – by placing a pattern piece to a fold instead, if the seam is merely a design feature and not an opening. Remember that it is the stitching line which goes to the fold and not the cutting line.

Placing yokes, pocket flaps and welts diagonally is a good idea. It avoids having to match them at all and it also looks good.

When tacking up a plaid or a stripe, slip tack from the right side, to ensure a perfect match. (See p. 39.)

### ► AN UNEVEN PLAID

To match an uneven plaid the fabric must be cut one way – that is, with all the pattern pieces lying in the same direction. Choose a pattern without too many pieces or construction seams.

The method outlined above will also be a help in placing an uneven plaid, but the most exact method of cutting out an uneven plaid is to cut it on *single* fabric, matching the notches in the seams and positioning dominant lines carefully, as above.

Open out the fabric and cut all the garment pieces once, matching the bars and balancing the design, as above. Keep the pattern pinned to the fabric and place it with the pattern face *downwards*, that is, the pattern between the fabric layers, to cut a second time. This way you can *see* that the plaid is matching.

Cutting out singly, this way, makes it very easy to cut an uneven plaid accurately, but you will need plenty of fabric as it is also wasteful.

## BORDERED FABRIC

Fabrics which have a design along one sel-

vedge only, defy all the rules in that they are most often cut using the selvedge around the body and not up and down. There are patterns designed specifically for borders, but you can adapt most patterns other than flared A-line skirts.

The most common way of using a border is at the skirt and sleeve hems. In these cases cut the hemlines straight, following the design, and not into the usual curve.

## FABRIC WITH A LARGE DESIGN

For these, avoid patterns with too many pieces and construction seams, and use a 'with nap' layout. Before you cut any fabric with a pronounced design, drape it over the entire body to 'place' the design. Large motifs usually look more pleasing placed in an irregular fashion, but it will depend on the actual design, so experiment with the fabric. Allow extra fabric for large design repeats. If you're unsure, ask the advice of the assistants in the shop, they should be able to help you.

## CUTTING OUT

Before you cut, check:

**1** the number of pattern pieces on your cutting layout against those on your fabric.
**2** that the grain arrows run parallel to the selvedge.
**3** that those pieces marked 'place to the fold of the fabric' are in the correct position.
**4** that shaded pattern pieces are face down, i.e. printed side down.
**5** whether the pattern piece is marked 'cut one' or 'cut four'.
**6** that any peculiarity of the fabric has been taken into account, i.e. one-way design, matching plaids etc.

Cut out the pattern using sharp, long-bladed scissors. Cut with the entire length of the blade using even strokes and making sure you keep exactly to the cutting line. Place one hand on the fabric next to and parallel with the shears as you cut. Don't lift the fabric up as this causes the pattern to shift. Cut out the main pieces, moving the fabric as little as possible. Avoid folding them as you stack them in a neat pile. Keep the largest pieces of leftover fabric and also a small square of fabric which you can staple to the pattern envelope. This will jog your memory if you use it again. Multi-sized patterns do not have a marked seam allowance so you must cut very accurately to obtain the correct stitching line. Cut the notches outwards so that you can see at a glance where the seams join and cut the double notch as one long notch. Cutting notches accurately makes joining the garment pieces together very much easier.

When there is a line on the pattern marked 'snip' which finishes with a large dot, it is a good idea to cut this line *almost* to the dot and then to oversew the raw edges at the cutting out stage. This gives a very accurate mark for an important construction detail and there will be no mistake if and when the pattern says 'clip to dot'. Note that 'clip'

means to cut (see the Dressmaker's Dictionary on p. 135).

A short clip in the top and bottom of the fold line is also a good idea as it establishes the exact position of the fold. Use this for pleats too, snipping only the fold and not the placement line of the pleat, to distinguish between the two.

## MARKING YOUR FABRIC

When you have cut out, do not remove the pattern until you have transferred as much information as you can from the tissue to the fabric. As you become a more experienced dressmaker you will find ways of making dressmaking quicker, but skipping the marking isn't one of them!

You may prefer to mark with carbon, tracing paper or a marking pencil, or to use one of the proprietary gadgets for tailor's tacking on the market, rather than using thread. It doesn't matter which method you use, as long as you do mark your fabric. This means that you can join up the pieces accurately and this is the only way to achieve a professional look to your home sewing.

## WAYS OF MARKING YOUR FABRIC

**11** Oversew the clip

### ▶ TAILOR'S TACKING

Use a long double thread and take a small stitch through the pattern symbol and both layers of fabric, making sure that you leave a long end. Take a second stitch in exactly the same spot and pull the thread through, forming a loop. Cut the thread so that you leave another long end. Tease the fabric layers apart and cut the thread between them so that you leave a tuft of thread on each side.

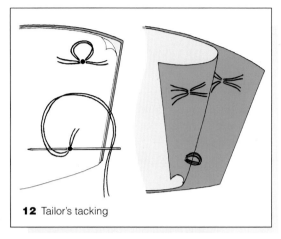

**12** Tailor's tacking

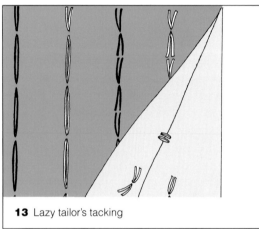

**13** Lazy tailor's tacking

the pattern as solid and broken lines. Cutting notches accurately makes joining the garment pieces together very much easier.

Smooth-textured fabric can be marked on the wrong side with dressmaker's coloured carbon paper and a tracing wheel, following the directions on the packet.

Always mark:
**1** Dots (distinguish between large and small dots with different colours of thread).
**2** Centre-front and centre-back, with a bold line of tacking stitches.
**3** Stitching and fold lines, such as those for pleats and trouser zips.
**4** Darts.
**5** The position for pockets and buttonholes.

After you have put in your tailor tacks and have removed the paper pattern it is a good idea, if you are a beginner, to label the fabric pieces. For example, a skirt which is made of many panels will have several pieces which are almost, but not quite, the same shape. So pin a small piece of paper to each piece identifying it as skirt side front, skirt front, skirt side back etc. It is also very helpful to identify the wrong side of the fabric when this is not immediately obvious. You can either use a label or tailor's chalk to do this. This means you can avoid making up two left sleeves and two right fronts!

You will find it a great help to mark the *exact* stitching line for setting in a sleeve and putting on a collar; it makes the task much simpler. With a multi-sized pattern the stitching line is not given, so cut out accurately and then mark the stitching line with a line of tacking 1.5 cm ($\frac{5}{8}$ in) from the cut edge, using a seam guide or tape measure.

Centre-front lines, pleats and tucks can be marked with thread, using a lazy tailor's tacking. This is the same as the above, but omitting the loop so it is quicker. Some of the thread may be lost with this method as the stitches are not as firmly anchored, but the remaining stitches can be joined up using a ruler and tailor's chalk. For pleats, use a different colour of thread for the fold lines from the placement lines, which are shown on

## CHAPTER FOUR

# STITCHING AND FINISHING

▷ *Machine stitching and finishing*

▷ *Hand stitching and finishing*

▷ *Pressing and shrinking hems and seams*

▷ *Interfacing, lining fabrics, shoulder pads, and their uses*

**M**ost of the construction of any garment is done by machine and, thankfully, the modern sewing machine is a joy to use. Your machine is probably capable of far more than you ask it to do, so read the instruction manual thoroughly to make sure that you are taking full advantage of it.

The construction seams are one of the most noticeable parts of any item of clothing, particularly on a plain fabric. They should appear as smooth, flattering lines, unpuckered and pressed absolutely flat. To achieve this, use a suitable size of machine stitch, between numbers 2 and 3 on most machines (10–12 stitches to the inch on older machines) and for most fabrics. A fine thread which 'sinks' into the fabric and a sharp machine needle are also essential.

It's a good idea to test a seam on a scrap of fabric. If the machine stitching is tight and causing puckering adjust the machine tension referring to your manual. If individual yarns of the fabric itself are being pulled in from the sides then the machine needle is blunt and needs replacing.

Make full use of the different stitches which are available on your machine. A stretch stitch is not only excellent for seams on stretch fabric, it is also very effective used as a bold top stitching on the right side of the fabric, to emphasise a seam on a shirt-type blouse, for example. Many machines have limited embroidery stitches but even these can look extremely professional when used with restraint. Several parallel rows of a self-colour embroidery (white on white, for example) can look very good on a blouse front and on the cuffs. Even the basic feather stitch can often be used in place of a line of straight stitching for attaching lace or for stitching the hem of a skirt lining.

When you finish a seam always turn the balance wheel of the sewing machine towards you so that you remove the fabric and cut the thread with the needle in its highest position. This means that the next movement of the needle is down so that it won't come unthreaded when you next start to sew. Today, all new machines are fitted with a reverse stitch which goes back over the end of the seam to secure the thread ends and to finish off a seam. It isn't always necessary to take time to do this, especially if the seam is going to be crossed by another. But it is important to do this with edges which may give when you are trying on and fitting the garment.

Shoulder seams should have a reverse stitch at both ends to stabilise the neck curve (for attaching the collar) and the shoulder seam (for inserting the sleeve). The wide end of a dart and the waist edges of skirt seams should also be finished with a reverse stitch. Do not, however, do a reverse stitch at the point of a dart or the lower end of a zip as this will look messy. Simply pull the ends of the thread through to the wrong side and knot them together.

Your sewing machine can save you a great deal of time-consuming hand sewing. The blind hem stitch is very useful on thick fabric and children's clothes although unfortunately, this stitch is not invisible enough for fine and plain fabric. The zig-zag stitch will neaten inside seam edges. Adjust this to a very narrow width for a really neat finish. An overlock-type stitch will stitch and neaten the seam in one operation, although it does not cut the fabric as the true overlock machine does.

As you will find when you experiment with your own model, the modern sewing machine is amazingly versatile. However, there are still some dressmaking procedures that you will have to do by hand – and it is these that we come to in this chapter.

# HAND SEWING

The hand stitches you will need in dress-making are:

## ▶ TACKING

This is not any old stitch, but a long and short stitch, which will hold the fabric pieces together for the purposes of fitting and which is better than large stitches of equal size.

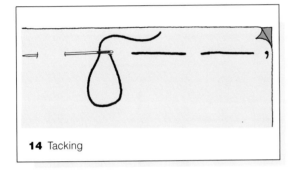

**14** Tacking

## ▶ DIAGONAL TACKING

Diagonal tacking holds pleats, gathers and overlaps in place.

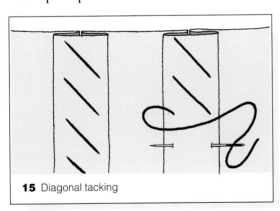

**15** Diagonal tacking

## ▶ SLIP TACKING

This is tacking from the *right* side and is the best way to deal with difficult patterns and checks. Press one seam allowance under and

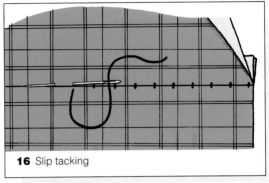

**16** Slip tacking

then position it correctly on top of the other seam line. Slip the needle alternately through the fold and then immediately below through the fabric.

## ▶ RUNNING STITCH

These are small, evenly sized and evenly spaced stitches which should be used as tacking for areas which require careful fitting, e.g. set-in sleeves.

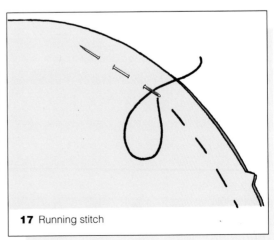

**17** Running stitch

## ▶ STAY STITCHING

Stay stitching is a line of small running stitches or machine stitches which is worked just above the stitching line round curved edges to prevent them stretching.

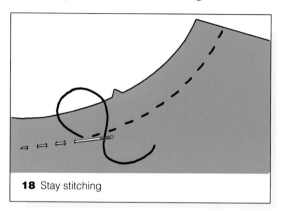

**18** Stay stitching

## ▶ PAD STITCH

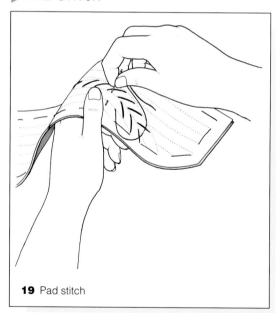

**19** Pad stitch

Pad stitches are small diagonal stitches worked in parallel rows, in a matching thread, to fuse canvas interfacing to an undercollar. Take a small stitch through canvas and fabric

(canvas uppermost) inserting the needle from right to left. The stitches on the fabric side are almost invisible.

## ▶ BACK STITCH

Back stitch is a firm hand stitch for awkward areas where machining is tricky, e.g. the overlap at the end of a waistband. Bring the needle out a stitch length beyond where the thread emerges. Insert it back again at the end of the previous stitch.

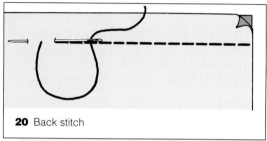

**20** Back stitch

## ▶ GATHERING STITCH

This is a *very* small version of a running stitch – the smaller the better. By far the best way to make evenly spaced gathers.

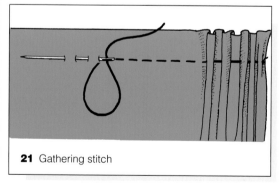

**21** Gathering stitch

## ▶ OVERSEWING

This is a method of sewing over two edges to bind them together. Oversewing is worked on a single edge to prevent fraying; it is sometimes referred to as overcasting. The needle can be inserted straight or slanting, which will affect the lie of the stitches.

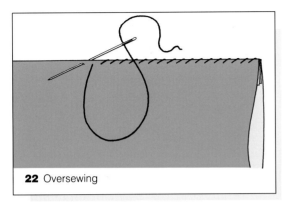

**22** Oversewing

## ▶CATCH STITCHING

An invisible stitch, worked loosely, taking up only a thread of fabric from top and bottom alternately, inside a hem or to hold the inner edge of sewn-in interfacing in place.

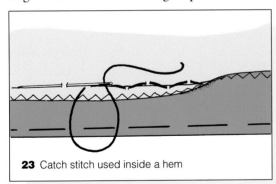

**23** Catch stitch used inside a hem

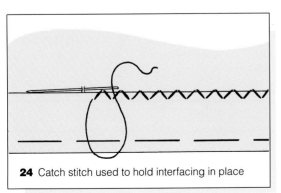

**24** Catch stitch used to hold interfacing in place

## ▶SLIP STITCHING

This is an invisible stitch used to draw two edges together invisibly, as in a hand-sewn lining. Slip the needle through the fold and, immediately below where the needle comes out, take a small stitch of the fabric. Re-insert the needle immediately above.

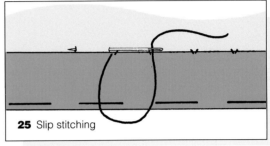

**25** Slip stitching

## ▶HAND HEMMING

An almost invisible stitch, hand hemming is worked from right to left with the hem draped over the fingers of the left hand. Pick up a thread from the fabric just below the folded edge of the hem, then a thread from the fold in the hem itself.

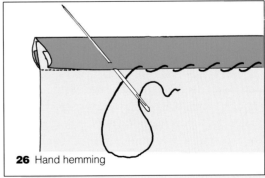

**26** Hand hemming

*41*

# PRESSING

Pressing is not ironing. It is an up and down, press and release movement, and an integral part of the process of creating clothes, because you cannot adequately press seams and edges once the pieces of fabric have been joined. As the heat tolerance of new mixtures of fibres is difficult to predict, it is important to test a scrap of your fabric before pressing any seams.

Some lightweight and sheer fabrics can be adequately pressed with a bare iron, but most fabrics are improved by pressing with a steam iron or a damp cloth and very often by a good pressing using both of these together.

## WHAT TO PRESS AND HOW TO PRESS IT

### ▶ SEAMS

The golden rule for pressing seams is: when you have stitched it, press it! First press the line of stitching, then open out the seam and, running your fingers down just in front of the toe of the iron, press down the length of the seam to open it. Press each open seam twice, first on the wrong side and then lightly on the right side.

Some types of fabric and in particular navy and black fabric may leave an imprint of the seam line on the right side. To prevent this, make a seam roll by covering a cardboard tube from the inside of a roll of dress fabric with an old piece of blanket. Press only the seam line over the curve of the roll, using the tip of the iron.

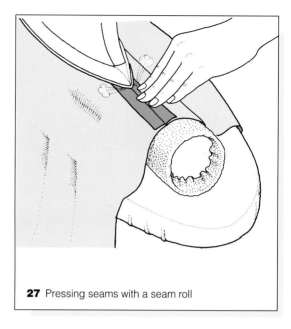

**27** Pressing seams with a seam roll

### ▶ DARTS

Press the stitching line, taking care not to press beyond the actual dart point. Then press the dart to one side; vertical darts towards the centre, horizontal darts downwards.

**28** Press darts in the correct direction

Then press on the right side of the dart using a cloth if necessary. Slip a piece of thin card between the fabric and the fold of the dart to prevent an imprint of the dart appearing on the right side.

On heavy fabrics and when the pattern indicates, slit the dart along the fold to within 1.5 cm ($\frac{5}{8}$ in) and press it open.

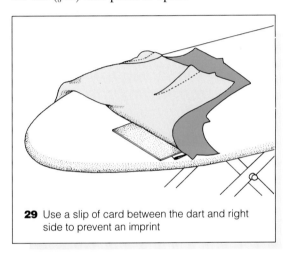

**29** Use a slip of card between the dart and right side to prevent an imprint

## ▶ GATHERS

Do not press gathers; it is the seam line into which the gathers are stitched that you press.

Draw the gathered fabric off the edge of the ironing board so that the seam is exactly on the edge with the gathers hanging down. Press the seam only, on both sides, with the point of the iron.

## ▶ HEMS

Never press a hem with the skirt draped round the ironing board as this tends to stretch the fabric. Arrange the finished hem so that it lies flat along the board and press only the fold. If for any reason you do need to press over the edge of the hem from the right side, then place a strip of the same fabric butting the edge of the hem on the inside to avoid forming a ridge.

Shrinking a hem in a wool or wool mixture will reduce the fullness in the hem-turning in, for example, a flared skirt. This is done at the seams using plenty of steam. Ease up the excess fullness each side of the seam with a gathering thread. Slip card between the hem and the fabric. Then using steam and a damp cloth over the point of the iron, hold the iron over the gathers until they become damp. Gently nudge the

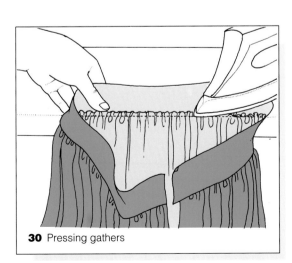

**30** Pressing gathers

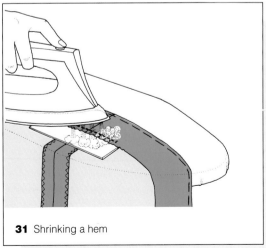

**31** Shrinking a hem

yarns together with the point of the iron until the fullness disappears. Press lightly to set the fabric and to dry it.

### ▶ PLEATS

Mark and tack the pleats accurately before they are pressed. As with the darts, slip thin card beneath the foldline of the pleat to prevent an imprint. Press on the right side first so that you can see that the pleats are set correctly. Cover as much of the pleated area at one time as you can with a damp muslin cloth laid over the pleats. Press heavily using steam and taking care not to move the fabric. Press again with a dry cloth and do not move the fabric until it is quite dry. Repeat the procedure on the wrong side. Remove the tacking only when the garment is completed and then press lightly on the right side to remove any imprint from the tacking.

### ▶ UNPRESSED PLEATS

As their name implies these pleats are not pressed-in heavily. Hang the dress or skirt from a skirt hanger so that the pleats are hanging correctly. Set the pleats by holding a steam iron very close to the folds and then allow them to dry in place.

### ▶ EDGES

It is essential to get flat crisp edges to achieve a professional look in dressmaking. First roll the seam line between the finger and thumb so that it is exactly on the edge. Tack close to the edge and press on the right side using a damp cloth, if necessary. Press on the wrong side and then remove the edge tacking. Finally, press again lightly on the right side to remove any imprint of the tacking.

### ▶ SLEEVES

A sleeve head is seldom improved by pressing though the underarm sleeve seams may be pressed open.

# INTERFACINGS

Clothes would not keep their structure without interfacings. They are used to stabilise and strengthen fabric as well as to shape it. New and better interfacings have simplified the job of dressmaking; but which one do you choose?

For dressmaking, the most dependable interfacing is non-woven and it comes in two forms: sew-in and iron-on. Each type comes in several weights, suitable for all types of fabric. A stretch interfacing is available for knit fabrics, which although they do not need to be stiffened, do need to be strengthened in some areas, e.g. buttonholes, and stabilised in others, e.g. collars and cuffs.

## SEW-IN OR IRON-ON?

Iron-on interfacing is a boon, it makes sewing quicker and usually gives good results – but not always. It is unsuitable for fabrics with a 'hairy' surface (it does not adhere properly) or for pile fabrics, such as corduroy which would mark with heavy pressing. Also it does not work well on acetates and some polyesters. If you are in doubt, buy sew-in interfacing. Iron-on is also at its best when restricted to small areas. Bear in mind that you can use a combination of the two and also vary the weights of interfacing used in the same garment.

In general, interfacing should be slightly lighter in weight than your fabric, to support it without dominating it. Before you buy it, drape the fabric over the interfacing and see if you like the effect. Always test iron-on interfacing on a scrap of fabric before using it on the garment pieces.

## APPLYING INTERFACING

Cut the interfacing using the paper pattern, snipping off all the corners at the stitching line. Stretch interfacing has a grain line but the other non-woven interfacings have not. Follow the pattern instructions as to which parts of the garments are to be interfaced.

### ▶ SEW-IN INTERFACING

Tack this a fraction outside the stitching line to the wrong side of the fabric. Trim away the surplus interfacing in the seam allowance, either before or after stitching the seam.

### ▶ IRON-ON INTERFACING

Mark the stitching line in pencil on the interfacing. With a multi-sized pattern, cut out accurately and mark the 1.5 cm ($\frac{5}{8}$ in) seam allowance from the edge on the interfacing.

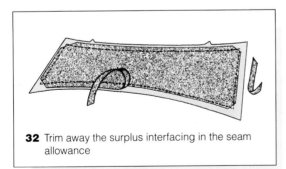

**32** Trim away the surplus interfacing in the seam allowance

Trim away the seam allowance. Fuse the interfacing to the fabric with a hot iron and a damp cloth. Press firmly, taking care not to move the fabric. Cover as large an area as you can each time and hold the iron, exerting

pressure, on each overlapping section for at least 15 seconds.

Neaten the edges of the neck and front facings with a small, neat zigzag or over-locking, stitching through interfacing and fabric together.

## LININGS

Linings are important because they add body and structure to clothes. Their purpose is not solely to make clothes easier to slip on and off or to hide inside seams. Whether your pattern gives a lining or not, as you progress in dressmaking you can use your own judgement as to whether the design, made up in your choice of fabric, would be improved by lining. Most dressmakers, for example, prefer to line a skirt. However, the lines of some fabric, e.g. jersey and crepe, may be destroyed by lining. The nature of the fabric is such that a solid lining may destroy the effect you are trying to create, such as draped and fluid lines. If you are uncertain, then complete the garment and try it on with a slip; you can always add a lining afterwards.

Lining fabric should be opaque and good quality. Most dressmakers tend to use the taffeta fabric sold as 'lining', which comes in a good colour range and is very adequate for the job, but if you want to give an extra special touch, you can use any fabric that is colourfast, anti-static, crease resistant and slippery. The lining must not be heavier than the fabric it lines. Silk and polyester silk-types, brocade, satin, Jacquard-woven and striped acetates all add interest used as linings. If you are making an outfit with a blouse and lined jacket or waistcoat, why not use the blouse fabric for the lining as well?

Lining may be taken right to the edge of a garment, or attached to a facing. It can be put in by hand or machine.

# SHOULDER PADS

On the back of the pattern envelope, you will find a brief description of the garment you are making with a line drawing which will give you an indication of the sleeve and armhole treatment. Extended shoulders give a wide shoulder outline, although the amount varies from one designer to another. Dropped shoulders are similar, but they curve after extending beyond the normal shoulder line and so give a softer silhouette than the extended shoulder, which is angular.

Fashion shoulders need pads. They are a tremendous asset to the home dressmaker because they give a sophisticated silhouette by adding width at the top, which helps to balance a plumper hipline and give an impression of height. They can also be very useful in correcting figure imbalances at the fitting stage.

Different shapes of pads are available for raglan sleeves, for sleeves cut in one with the bodice and for set-in sleeves. They are available in small, medium and large. Small, thin, shaped pads are also available for filling out sleeve heads and shoulder shapers are available for filling in the hollow at the front of a shoulder. The method of inserting a shoulder pad is described on p. 89.

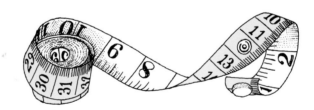

## CHAPTER FIVE

# SKIRTS

▷ *Fitting a skirt*

▷ *Pleats*

▷ *Skirt pockets*

▷ *Putting in a skirt zip*

▷ *Lining a skirt*

▷ *Attaching a waistband*

▷ *Hemming a skirt*

A skirt is usually the first item that the new home dressmaker chooses to make. It is simple, easy to wear and is the one garment that many women can never have too many of in the wardrobe.

Looking through the skirt section of the pattern catalogue is a delight. There are flared and gored skirts, panelled, wrap, circular, pleated, straight, draped, bias cut and gathered skirts. They come in knee length, mini, ankle, calf and floor length and can be made in checked, floral, striped, spotted, plain and tartan fabrics. Is it any wonder that we take so long to choose?

If you look carefully through this section you will find that many of the patterns include several variations of the design in the one pattern. This is a good buy and will encourage you to make up the pattern again in a different sort of fabric incorporating the slight design variations in the different patterns.

A complete beginner should choose a simple design – one with few construction seams. A skirt showing a number of panels or a skirt on a hip basque is going to have several more pieces and therefore more seams to join. An A-line skirt will have fewer pattern pieces to contend with. Wrap skirts and gathered skirts are easy to make, pleated and button-through skirts are a little more difficult.

The hem length is a very important part of the total silhouette and the overall look of an outfit. Fashion dictates the hem length to a certain degree, but use your eye to judge both the balance of the hemline in relation to the width at the hip and the effect of the complete outfit worn with shoes and tights. An extra half-inch or two can make all the difference. A more graceful line is usually achieved with a longer length, but if the skirt is fashionably short, the same effect can be achieved either by wearing a top and skirt of the same colour or, if the top is in a contrast colour, by wearing tights which are the same colour as the top.

To sew a skirt successfully, make sure you have your correct pattern size (see p. 17) and check the standard pattern measurements with your own, including the length. Adjust your pattern as necessary (see p. 29). Cut out the pieces, taking care with a plaid fabric (see p. 32) and before you start to stitch, tack up the skirt seams and any darts and pleats. Also, pin on the waistband for a first fitting. Make a line of tacking down the straight grain at the centre-front and centre-back of the skirt.

# FITTING A SKIRT

The commonest fitting problems are, fortunately, also the easiest to deal with. Experiment at this stage with the fitting. Fitting is a personal thing and the only way to make your clothes fit you the way you want them to is to have the confidence to try out fabric adjustments at this stage.

### ▶ WRINKLES BELOW THE BACK WAISTBAND

If the fabric is forming into folds just below the back waistband only, this is caused by a hollow back, sometimes called a sway back. Remove the waistband at the back and ease up the skirt waist. A small adjustment of 12 mm ($\frac{1}{2}$ in) can make all the difference, but experiment until the wrinkles disappear. You may also have to adjust the length of the darts once you have taken up the fabric at the back.

### ▶ WRINKLES UNDERNEATH THE WHOLE WAISTBAND

This often occurs once the waistband has been stitched on. The waistband fits well, the rest of the skirt is, apparently, a good fit, but the fabric wrinkles just below the band. This is because the skirt itself is too tight over the high part of the hips and cannot fall down over the hips, because it is 'sitting' on the hips.

Remove the band, let out the curve of the side seam and/or the darts sufficiently to allow the skirt to drop freely from the waistband.

### ▶ THE SKIRT IS NOT HANGING STRAIGHT

The easiest way to check whether the skirt hangs straight is to check whether the centre-front or centre-back tacking line is hanging vertically. If not, it means that you have one hip higher than the other. Remove the waist-

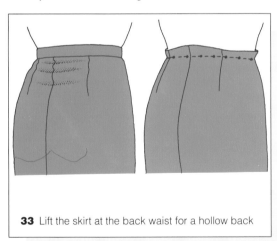

**33** Lift the skirt at the back waist for a hollow back

**34** Lift the skirt side until the centre line is vertical

band and drop the skirt on the short side and/or lift the other side until the centre line hangs straight and the hem is parallel to the floor. You will have to let out the side seam a little too.

These problems are not usually evident until the fitting stage. If you come across any of these, go back to the paper pattern and make the same adjustment on the tissue, so that the pattern is ready for use the next time you want it.

# PLEATS

Skirt pleats should also be dealt with before any permanent stitching is done.

Thread-mark the dots accurately, using different colours of thread to denote the placement and fold lines (see p. 36). Pick up the pleats from the right side and pin the fold through all the thicknesses. Tack with diagonal tacking to hold. When all the pleats are placed, tack along the top edge with diagonal tacking (see p. 39). Press well, if necessary using card underneath the pleat edge to prevent an imprint on the right side.

It is quite simple to add a pleat to a plain skirt pattern. Draw the position of the pleat on the pattern. Cut the paper on this line. Decide on the depth of pleat (heavier fabric will need deeper pleats) then make up the actual pleat just as you would like it, in thin paper (you will need twice the required depth of pleat). Fold the paper to the correct size and tape the pleat and pattern together.

If your fabric is not wide enough to accommodate the amount of pleat all in one, you can still add one, but you will need to join it with a separate pleat underlay, that is, a strip of extra fabric stitched to the underside to form a pleat.

Pleats can be held by stitching from the inside if you do not want any top-stitching, e.g. a silk or delicate fabric.

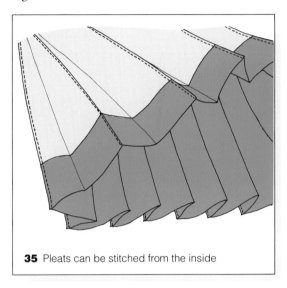

**35** Pleats can be stitched from the inside

On linen-types and heavier fabric, a bold top-stitching on the outside is appropriate. Most pleats are improved by edge-stitching, on the inside or the outside, right at the very edge in a good match of thread.

# SKIRT POCKETS

Skirt pockets set into the side seam are stitched as one continuous seam. They are simple to make and you can add this type of pocket to any skirt whether the pattern gives a side-seam pocket or not.

It is done in two ways. The pocket can be made from two separate pieces of fabric attached to the side seam. This way, if the skirt fabric is thick, lining fabric can be substituted for one or both pieces. The pocket can also be made by extending the side seam into a pocket shape.

If the pattern does not include a pocket pattern, cut a paper pattern to the shape given from a piece of paper, measuring 25.5 cm (10½ ins) by 18 cm (7 ins).

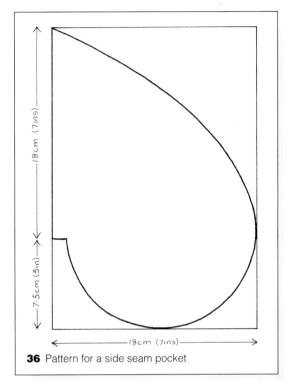

**36** Pattern for a side seam pocket

above and below the pocket so that the seam can be pressed open. Press the pocket towards the front seam.

If you have enough fabric you can cut the pocket as part of the skirt pieces. You will

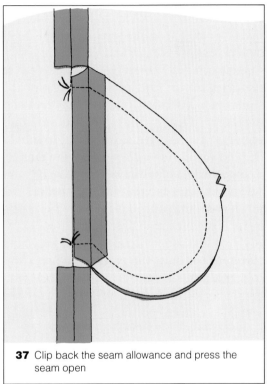

**37** Clip back the seam allowance and press the seam open

When the pattern includes a seam pocket, the seam also has an extension, i.e. the seam allowance is extended at the point where the pocket is inserted into the seam. When adding a pocket yourself, there will be no side-seam extension, so stitch the pocket pieces to the seams taking only half the usual seam allowance. On bias seams and stretch fabrics, re-inforce the seam by including narrow seam tape in the stitching line.

Stitch the side seams of the skirt in one continuous seam and pivot the fabric while the needle is still in it when you reach the join of the pockets. Clip the back seam allowance

therefore not need the seam allowances which have been given to attach the pocket pieces. Pin the pocket piece from the pattern over the side seam of the skirt or trouser pattern piece, placing the stitching lines of the pattern pieces on top of one another. Pin and cut the pocket as one with the skirt.

# THE ZIP

A skirt zip should look like the continuation of the seam line: it should be invisible. It should not show the tape or the zip pull at all and the line of top-stitching should be completely straight. The following method makes putting in a zip very easy, but don't be tempted to take any short cuts!

First stitch the centre-back seam as far as the mark for the zip, leaving the rest of the seam open. Tack down the folded edges and press them. Position the zip with the zip pull uppermost and keep it closed. The zip should be positioned so that the edge of the teeth is against the fold of the fabric on the right hand side of the seam and the zip pull is 6 mm ($\frac{1}{4}$ in) down from the stitching line for the waistband. Tack the zip in position.

Using the zipper foot on your machine (this foot has only one prong) stitch as close as you can to the fold of the fabric and to the teeth of the zip.

Bring the other side of the zip opening over to completely conceal the zip itself, with the folded edge lying on top of the line of machine stitching you have just completed. The edges will overlap just a fraction at this stage. Tack the folded edge in place securely, using short diagonal tacking stitches.

To make sure you get the final stitching of the zip absolutely straight first time, make a guideline to follow in contrasting thread, parallel to the folded edge and 8 mm ($\frac{3}{8}$ in) away from it.

Using the zipper foot, stitch the zip, following the guide line and stitch across the end of the zip at an angle. Remove the tacking and guide line and press the zip.

Although the method I have just described is by far the easiest way to put in a zip, in fine fabric you may want to have no line of

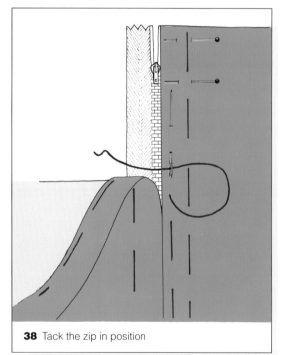

**38** Tack the zip in position

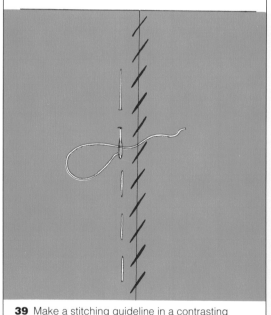

**39** Make a stitching guideline in a contrasting thread

machine stitching on the right side at all and so you need to put in the zip by hand.

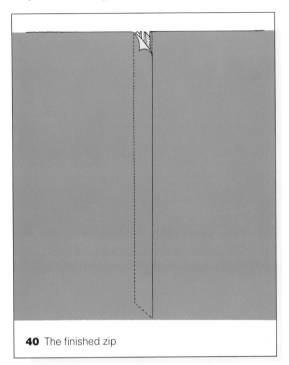

**40** The finished zip

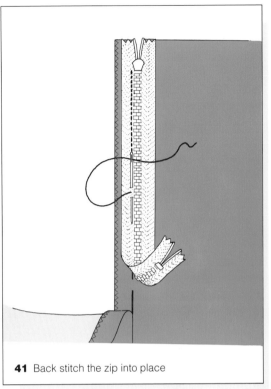

**41** Back stitch the zip into place

## PUTTING IN A ZIP BY HAND

Fold back the seam allowance on the left hand side of the skirt only. On the right hand side, mark the seam line with tacking stitches.

Place the skirt flat with the right side uppermost. Position the zip with the zip pull facing downwards on the right hand seam allowance and the edge of the teeth next to the line of tacking. Make sure that the zip pull is 6 mm ($\frac{1}{4}$ in) down from the waist stitching line, as before, and then tack it into place. Stitch, using a back stitch (see p. 40).

Turn the zip to the right side and tack back the seam turning on that edge. Bring the other side of the zip-opening over to close the seam and completely conceal the zip.

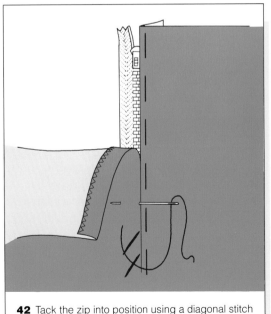

**42** Tack the zip into position using a diagonal stitch

Tack securely with diagonal tacking. Make a guideline for the final stitching, as in fig. 42.

Using a fine thread and a very small needle, complete the top stitching of the zip with a half backstitch. Do not take the needle back to the previous stitch, but insert it just behind where it emerges from the fabric. Then bring the needle out just in front of the thread. The stitches are small dots and are virtually invisible. For a centred zip see p. 87.

# LINING A SKIRT

Lining a skirt makes it move and hang better, which is why most home dressmakers prefer to line a skirt. However, draped, bias cut and figure hugging styles – where the fabric is intended to cling to the body – are better left unlined, as the lining will alter the properties of the fabric and the look of the skirt, e.g. a skirt cut in panels to make it flare at the hem with godet inserts gives a slim, curvy silhouette and should not be lined.

A skirt can be half lined, which means that the lining is shortened to above the knee, or sometimes just the skirt seat can be lined. This is done to keep the shape of the skirt in a fabric where a full lining is not suitable, e.g. soft or stretchy knits.

To line the seat of a skirt, cut out the lining using the back skirt pattern from the waist to below the widest part of the hips. Finish the hem of the lining. Place the lining flat on the inside of the skirt back and attach with diagonal tacking. It is then included in the stitching of the side seams.

A fully-lined skirt is cut from the same skirt pattern, omitting any pleats, pockets etc. Pin in the pleats on the pattern. If the skirt then lacks width at the hem, leave a side slit

in the lining for movement. Excess fullness in the width of an A-line skirt can also be pinned-in to make the side seams less shaped. Use your judgement. The idea is to use the same skirt pattern so that the lining skirt fits the outer skirt at the waist and hip but does away with unnecessary design features so that you are left with the basic skirt shape.

If you are using a very complicated pattern, an all-round pleated skirt or a flared skirt in eight panels, for example, then use a pattern for a straight skirt for the lining.

Ideally, knits and stretch fabric, if they are lined at all, should have linings of the same type of fabric. The easiest way to line jersey is to buy a waist slip in single jersey and to use that. Cut off the waist elastic and you have a ready-made, lace-edged skirt lining.

## TO ATTACH A SKIRT LINING

Make up the skirt and the lining as far as the zip. With the skirt wrong side out and the

**43** A fully-lined skirt

lining right side out, slip the lining over the skirt. Tack them together at the waist, matching the side seams and darts. Slip stitch the seam-turning down on to the zip tape.

Finish the skirt lining once the skirt hem has been finished, making it 2.5 cm (1 in) shorter than the skirt. The lining hem can be neatened with lace or machine embroidery.

# THE WAISTBAND

Putting a waistband on a skirt has been made much simpler by the wide range of waistband interfacings now on the market. Some of these interface both sides of the band and give a perforated stitching-line to follow. Others interface one side of the band only and are available as sew-in or iron-on. All waistband interfacings are available in several widths and weights. Experiment with the various types to find which type you prefer, as the firmness of the skirt band is a matter of personal choice as well as being related to the fabric weight.

Interface the band before attaching it to the skirt. Fold the band in half and press in the fold wrong sides together. Tack or fuse the interfacing to the wrong side of the band

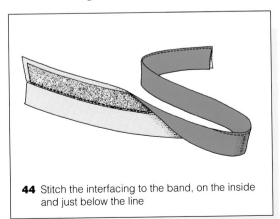

**44** Stitch the interfacing to the band, on the inside and just below the line

and stitch just below the fold line along the length of the band. This stitched line will be to the inside of the band, that is, against the body on the finished skirt, and is a good idea even if you use iron-on interfacing as it keeps it firmly in place.

Turn the seam allowance over the interfacing on the inner edge of the band.

## ATTACHING THE BAND

Work with the skirt right side out and position the raw edge of the band to the waist edge, right sides together. Allow a 1.5 cm ($\frac{5}{8}$ in) overlap at one end of the band and approx 3 cm ($1\frac{1}{4}$ in) at the other. It gives a neater finish if the longer overlap is on the underneath, that is, the skirt back, on a side zip.

Stitch the seam from the waistband side and trim the seam turnings to 6 mm ($\frac{1}{4}$ in) and trim away any interfacing to the seam line.

Fold the end back on itself, right sides together, and stitch across the end.

Trim the seam, cut off the corners and then turn right side out. Oversew the open edges of the overlap.

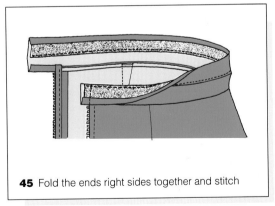

**45** Fold the ends right sides together and stitch

## A PARTLY ELASTICATED WAISTBAND

If you tend to fluctuate in size around the waist, you can substitute a length of wide firm elastic for part of the interfacing at the skirt back. This will ease the waistband into slight gathers at the centre back and will give you a little leeway with the waist size for a comfortable skirt, which is going to be worn under a sweater or jacket.

Make the skirt waist an easy fit. Make up the waist band to fit the skirt, then cut a strip of elastic the same width as the finished band to 25 cm (10 in) in length. Centre the strip of elastic at the centre-back of the waistband. Cut the interfacing to the length of the rest of the waistband, less 2.5 cm (1 in). Join it to the strip of elastic at the back.

Attach the interfacing to the band each side of the elastic in the usual way. Do not stitch the elastic to the band. The length of elastic can be adjusted as necessary.

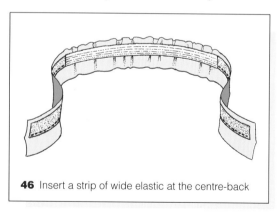

**46** Insert a strip of wide elastic at the centre-back

Alternatively, use wide elastic, elasticized facing, or elastic waistbanding as a waist-band facing, that is, for the inside of the band all the way round. The outside of the band is fabric, the inside is elastic. The elastic is kept just a little down from the top folded edge of the waistband so that it does not show. It allows slight adjustment and also gives a good grip as the inside 'lining' of elastic keeps the shirt firmly tucked in. The waistband is not interfaced as the elastic acts as the stiffening.

## THE HEM

The best way to get a straight hemline is to get help to measure it. Use a hem marker, stand on a table and stand still while someone measures the skirt length all the way round.

First decide on the finished length for your skirt while wearing the height of heel you will usually wear with the skirt. Put in one pin to mark the length and then get someone to move round you putting in pins at that distance from the table and about 8 cm (3 in) apart, whilst you stand still.

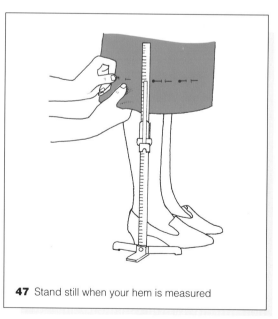

**47** Stand still when your hem is measured

Next, take off the skirt, lay it flat on the table and join up the pins with a line of chalk. Turn up the hem on that line and tack it on the edge. Press very lightly and then try it on to give a final check to the length.

When you are happy that the length is right, trim the inside hem – turning it up to 5 cm (2 in) for straight and A-line skirts, or less for bulky fabrics; 4 cm ($1\frac{1}{2}$ in) for flared skirts and 1.5 cm ($\frac{5}{8}$ in) for very flared and circular skirts. As a general guide, the more fullness there is in a hem, the more the turning must be reduced on the inside.

Neaten the hem edge with a small zigzag, then tack it up 6 mm ($\frac{1}{4}$ in) from the neatened edge. Turn the hem back on itself and work from the inside to catch stitch it in place (see p. 41).

A very narrow hem on a full or circular skirt can be finished by top-stitching by

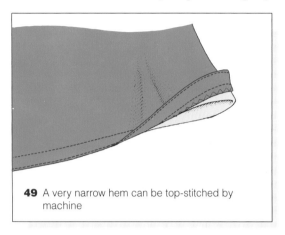

**49** A very narrow hem can be top-stitched by machine

machine. Make the first row of stitches on the very edge of the hem, working from the right side. Work a second row 6 mm ($\frac{1}{4}$ in) away from the first.

A hem in a pleated skirt in a thick fabric can be finished in two ways. It is usually easier and neater to leave the seams open at the hem, to turn up and stitch the hem and then stitch the remaining length of the pleat. Trim the seam to 6 mm ($\frac{1}{4}$ in), cut off the corner at the hem and neaten with a small zigzag or overlock stitch.

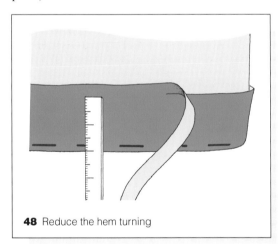

**48** Reduce the hem turning

If the hem is very flared you will have excess fullness at the seams. Work a row of gathering stitches (see p. 40) each side of the seam line and ease up the fullness, so that the hem lies flat and the seam lines are together.

In a pure wool fabric this surplus fabric can be shrunk so that the hem is completely flat (see p. 43).

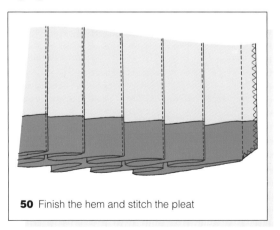

**50** Finish the hem and stitch the pleat

If you stitch the pleats first, clip the seam allowance at the edge of the hem and edge stitch the inside of the pleat close to the fold.

Above all, aim to keep your hem neat and inconspicuous so as not to draw attention away from the line and silhouette of your finished garment. Your skill with getting your hem right will definitely improve with practice.

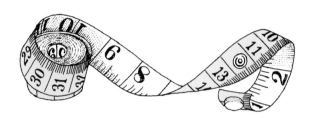

## CHAPTER SIX

# TROUSERS AND CULOTTES

*Fitting a pair of trousers or culottes*

*Inserting a trouser zip*

*Lining trousers*

There are so many styles of trousers these days that it is possible for everyone to find a pair to suit their figure: tight-fitting ones with tapered legs, styles which have softly pleated waists and which narrow at the ankles, baggy trousers which are full in the leg and gathered at the ankle, culottes with straight legs, and culottes which are so wide that they are simply a divided skirt. And who would have guessed that shorts would be in the pattern catalogues again to be made up in sequined fabric for evening wear?

The length of the finished trousers, culottes or shorts will depend upon your figure. A longer length will have the effect of making you look taller, so if you're short, keep your trousers really long so that the hems cover the tops of your shoes. Cropped trousers which finish at the calf or knee are flattering for those with slim ankles and more height. It's worth bearing in mind the fact that a pleated waistline often has the effect of slimming the figure where tight-fitting trousers emphasise it. Leggings look very effective worn with baggy jumpers and loose fitting shirts – a popular and attractive style for anyone who is trying to hide their bulges! So, before you buy your trousers, shorts or culottes pattern, think about the effect you would like to achieve.

Trousers are not difficult to make. The seams and zip are no more complex than those on a skirt. However, they can be difficult to fit. The shape of the trouser leg is not the problem, it is making the trousers fit neatly around the body (i.e. the bottom and tummy) that is difficult.

The best way to achieve a good fit is to tackle the problem in stages. First, take all the necessary measurements accurately. Then choose your best pattern size realistically (not hopefully!) by your *hip* measurement. This is because it is much easier to alter the waist than the hip. Next, measure and adjust this pattern to your own proportions (see pp. 61–63).

Before you cut out the trouser pattern pieces in your chosen fabric, cut them out and tack them up in a cheap fabric or even an old sheet. (This is not usually necessary for culottes which are loosely fitting anyway.) You can then fit this dummy pair of trousers to your figure and can use it to adjust your paper pattern *before* you cut out your good fabric. You will then have a trouser pattern that fits well and which you can confidently make up in a superb fabric, such as a fine wool for winter or a linen-type fabric for summer.

# FITTING TROUSERS

## STAGE 1

### ▶MEASURING UP

**The crotch depth** – This is the distance between the waist and the bottom of the hip. It is measured, seated on a chair, from the side waist to the chair seat. Trousers which pull down and away from the back waist on sitting down are too short in the 'rise', i.e. crotch depth.

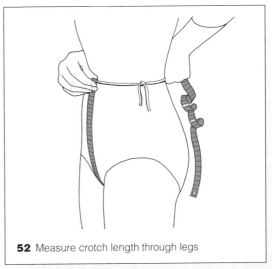

**52** Measure crotch length through legs

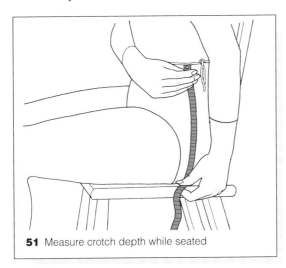

**51** Measure crotch depth while seated

Ease must be added to the crotch measurement before it is compared to the paper pattern. This varies according to the style of the trousers and fashion trends. The important thing is that the crotch depth is not too short. Add on the minimum ease, which is 1.3 cm ($\frac{1}{2}$ in).

**The crotch length** – This is the length of the trouser seam which goes through from front waist to back waist between the thighs. This seam can be adjusted at the front or back to give extra room when necessary. Add on the minimum ease, which is 2 cm ($\frac{3}{4}$ in).

The other measurements you need are waist, hip, thigh (this is only necessary if you have very plump thighs, and make sure you measure round the fattest part) and the trouser side length. Measure this from the side waist to the desired length at the ankle.

Fill in your measurements, add the ease and then compare them with the pattern and make a note of the adjustment needed.

## STAGE 2

### ▶COMPARING YOUR MEASUREMENTS WITH THE PATTERN

The crotch depth on the pattern is measured from the waist seam to the crotch line. If there is no marked line on your pattern, draw it in across the pattern at right angles to the grain line at the widest point. The crotch length is measured along the seam line, adding front and back seam lengths together. Stand the tape on its edge for accuracy.

Compare the thigh measurement on the pattern in the same place as you measured your own thighs. Allow for ease, which varies

|  | MINE | ADD MIN. EASE | TOTAL | PATTERN | ADJUSTMENT | |
|---|---|---|---|---|---|---|
|  |  |  |  |  | PLUS | MINUS |
| CROTCH DEPTH |  |  |  |  |  |  |
| CROTCH LENGTH |  |  |  |  |  |  |
| WAIST |  |  |  |  |  |  |
| HIPS (at widest point) |  |  |  |  |  |  |
| THIGH (around fullest part) |  |  |  |  |  |  |
| TROUSER LENGTH (from side waist to finished length) |  |  |  |  |  |  |

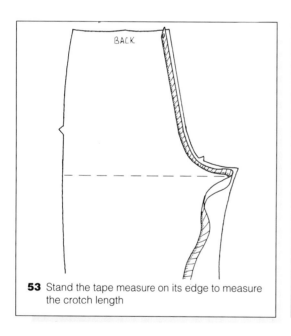

**53** Stand the tape measure on its edge to measure the crotch length

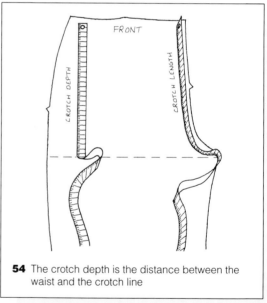

**54** The crotch depth is the distance between the waist and the crotch line

greatly according to the style of trousers. This rarely needs alteration unless your thighs are exceptionally plump.

## ▶ ADJUSTING THE TROUSER PATTERN TO YOUR OWN MEASUREMENTS

The crotch depth should be altered first.

**To shorten crotch depth** – There is a line marked on the pattern indicating where alterations must be made. Measure up from this line the amount you need to shorten the pattern and draw a line across, parallel to it. Fold the paper bringing the two lines together and pin in place.

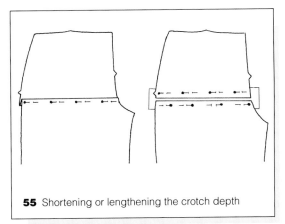

**55** Shortening or lengthening the crotch depth

**To lengthen crotch length** – Pin paper underneath the edge of the pattern. Measure the seam as before and extend the curve of the crotch by the desired amount. Re-draw the crotch curve, tapering in gradually to the original line.

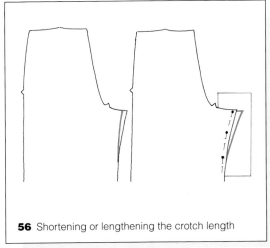

**56** Shortening or lengthening the crotch length

**To lengthen crotch depth** – Cut along the line indicated. Pin a strip of paper to one edge. Spread the pieces apart by the amount you need to add on and pin the other piece in place.

Re-measure the crotch length on the pattern if the crotch depth has been adjusted, because any further alteration may not be needed. However, for a large stomach or a flat bottom, further adjustment may be necessary.

To alter the crotch length, you will have to exercise judgement as to where the adjustment is needed – the front or the back pattern piece. If your figure is in proportion, then divide the alteration equally between front and back. Or, add more to the back than the front or vice versa, depending on where you need the extra fullness.

**To shorten crotch length** – Measure from the waist to the required amount on the crotch seam, standing the tape on edge. Draw in the crotch curve following the shape of the original curve and gradually tapering to join the original line.

As you will buy your pattern by your hip size you may find you need to adjust the waist measurement if your waist is smaller or larger than your hip size. With multi-sized patterns, the waist can be altered by gradually changing to the appropriate cutting line above the hip.

# STAGE 3

## ▶ FITTING THE TROUSERS

Careful pattern measurement and alteration minimises fitting, but when the pattern is made up into your chosen fabric, other small problems may come to light. Complete the try-out pair of trousers – include the zip, tack on the waistband, pin the hem to the correct length and then try them on.

If you have followed the above procedures carefully, you may be highly delighted with the fit. If you are not, or if you do not like any feature of them, the width at the ankle for example, don't hesitate to experiment with altering the trousers to please you. This is the stage for learning more about fitting – the trial and error stage.

Here are some of the things to look for and the ways to alter them. If you do make further alterations at the fitting stage, then go back to your paper pattern and make the same alterations on your pattern, by the method shown. You will then have the perfect trouser pattern that you can make up with confidence in any fabric.

### ▶ TROUBLE BEHIND

The commonest fault in trousers is wrinkling and excess fullness below the seat. If you have measured and adjusted before cutting out, as instructed, this will not be your problem; but it is included here for anyone who has started on a pair of trousers, without doing the appropriate measuring and has turned to this book for help!

If trousers sag below the bottom, remove the waistband and then raise the waistline

seam to take away the fullness. Take any extra width into the side seams and take in the darts to make the waist fit neatly.

If trousers strain and wrinkle below the seat it means that they are too tight in that area. Remove the waistband and let the waist seam drop.

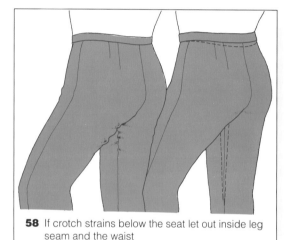

**58** If crotch strains below the seat let out inside leg seam and the waist

### ▶ TROUBLE IN FRONT

If there is any tightness and strain on the fabric over the stomach, remove the waistband, allow the front waistline to drop and let out each side seam and the front seam as necessary.

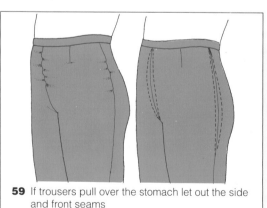

**59** If trousers pull over the stomach let out the side and front seams

**57** If trousers sag below the seat, raise the waist

# MAKING UP THE TROUSERS

The best stage to establish the position of the crease, if there is one, is after the stitching of the darts. Fold the individual legs in half, as shown, and lightly press in the position of the crease. Take the crease to the end of the dart in the front trouser and to the crotch point on the back.

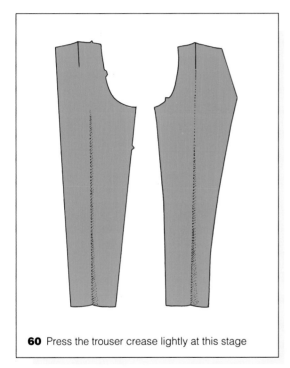

**60** Press the trouser crease lightly at this stage

In most cases this will be the correct position for the crease. In a very few cases, depending on the cut of the trouser you may need to move the crease a little towards the front, so don't press too heavily at this stage. Give the final pressing to the crease once the hem is finished. The edge can then be stitched with a fine machine-stitch in a perfect match of thread to hold the crease.

# INSERTING A TROUSER ZIP

This type of zip is easy and satisfying to insert, provided you mark all the relevant seam and fold lines. On women's clothes the right side laps over the left and the neatest way is to keep the zip completely concealed below the overlap by allowing slightly more on the left seam extension.

First, mark the large dot which indicates the start of the zip. Then mark the curve of the top stitching line on the *right front*, then both the centre-front lines (using a different colour of thread from the top-stitching).

Tack the centre-front seam of the trousers and machine stitch it only from the notch as far as the marked dot, using the triple strength stretch stitch on your machine (or do a double row of stitching). On the left side, clip the

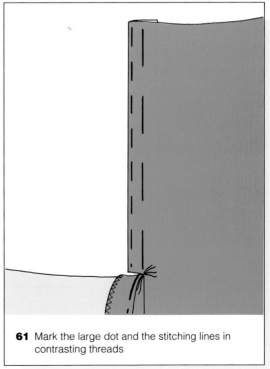

**61** Mark the large dot and the stitching lines in contrasting threads

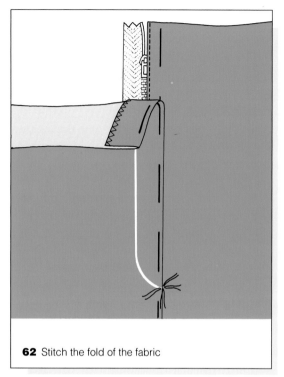

**62** Stitch the fold of the fabric

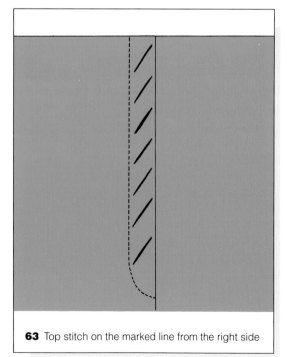

**63** Top stitch on the marked line from the right side

seam allowance almost to the dot, and oversew the raw edges.

On the right side, tack the zip extension to the inside on the centre-front line. On the left side, turn under the zip extension 6 mm ($\frac{1}{4}$ in) away from the centre line. Tack it on the edge and press the fold.

Place the closed zip under the left front edge, with the teeth just touching the tacked edge and the zip pull 2 cm ($\frac{3}{4}$ in) from the top edge. Using the zipper foot on your machine, stitch exactly on the fold of the fabric.

Close the opening by bringing the centre-front lines together. Tack with diagonal tacking through all thicknesses. Using the zipper foot, top-stitch on the marked line from the right side.

# LINING TROUSERS

For extra warmth and comfort it is quite easy to half-line trousers. Use a slippery, good quality lining, because the seam will take a good deal of strain.

Cut the lining to exactly the same pattern as the trouser fabric, using the paper pattern. Cut it across the leg at the length you want the lining to be. This can be to the knee or just below the seat.

Stitch the lining in the same way as the trousers themselves, but take slightly less into each seam, about 3 mm ($\frac{1}{8}$ in) less, so that the fit of the lining is easier than the trousers. Take the extra fullness at the waist into small pleats. Finish the lower edge of the lining with a small zigzag, rather than a narrow hem, which may show as a ridge. Tack the lining into the trousers before the waistband is added. Slip stitch the lining down on the zip tape.

## CHAPTER SEVEN

# *B*LOUSES AND SHIRTS

▶ *Seaming detail*

▶ *Attaching frills or ruffles*

▶ *Attaching a collar*

▶ *Making cuffs*

▶ *Setting in a sleeve*

Getting just the right top to match an outfit is easy for the home dressmaker. There are so many delightful blouse and shirt patterns to choose from: tailored shirt blouses, feminine blouses with ruffles and bows, baggy shirts and figure-hugging jersey tops. You can also make camisoles, body suits, sleeveless tops and backless waistcoats – the range seems endless.

Whichever style you select, the fabric is all-important. Refer to the back of the pattern envelope for fabrics suggested by the designer so that you can get the correct weight of fabric and interpret the 'look' of the illustration as closely as possible. A baggy shirt made up in a brightly checked cotton is going to give a completely different look from the same pattern made up in a lightweight voile. The first you can wear with jeans, the second as evening wear or over a swimsuit.

When you are working with fine fabric, seams and stitches become more evident. Using any old thread with whatever size of needle happens to be in the machine is no longer good enough! The seams must be given more attention as they are not only more conspicuous, but must stand up to wash and wear. The thread must sink into the fabric of the seam, so a fine needle and the correct thread are essential if you are to achieve the best results.

Don't shy away from making shirts and blouses – once you've mastered a few basic techniques you'll find them easy. A basic pattern can be varied in so many ways to give you a selection of quite different blouses, also today, there are so many patterns to choose from that you can avoid the trickier techniques involved in adding cuffs and collars and still make a sophisticated blouse or casual shirt before moving on to more complex patterns and fabrics. Shirts and blouses are definitely worth your time and effort.

# SEAMING DETAILS

Always make sure that you have the best thread and needle size for the fabric you are using. Ask the advice of an assistant if you're unsure.

Before you start to sew, test a seam on a double layer of fabric. Make a fairly long seam and press it open. The right side should be perfectly flat and wrinkle free.

On cotton and sturdy fabric the seam edges of an open seam can be neatened with small seam turning and a stitched edge or with a very small zigzag. Experiment with the stitch length and width until you have a really fine edge.

Shirt-type blouses in sturdy fabric look smart with top-stitched yokes and shoulder seams. Both seam turnings are pressed in the same direction (towards the yoke or as indicated in the pattern) and stitched 6 mm ($\frac{1}{4}$ in) from the seam line.

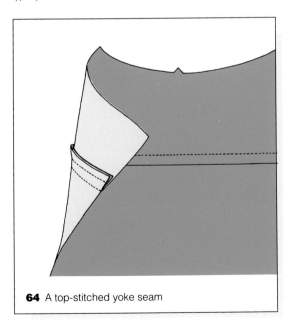

**64** A top-stitched yoke seam

Seams for a shirt-style blouse can also be overlapped at the stitching line and stitched on the right side close to the fold of the fabric.

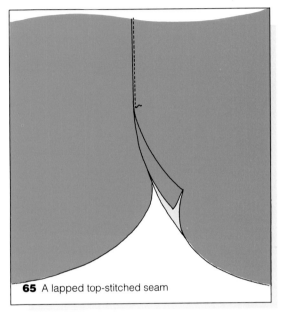

**65** A lapped top-stitched seam

You can make a much finer seam on sheer fabric. Do not press the seams open. First stitch the seam and then trim both turnings together to 6 mm ($\frac{1}{4}$ in) or less and zigzag both edges together with a small stitch.

If you are making a style which requires no fitting, such as an oversized shirt blouse, you can stitch and neaten the seam in the one operation on most modern sewing machines.

# FRILLS AND RUFFLES

Once the main blouse seams are stitched, fashion details such as frills or ruffles in the front bands or edges are included.

Frills or ruffles come and go with fashion, but it is easy to add ruffles to a pattern if you cannot find exactly the design you want.

## ▶ A CIRCULAR RUFFLE

A waterfall effect is achieved by cutting a frill from a circle of fabric. To cut a circular ruffle

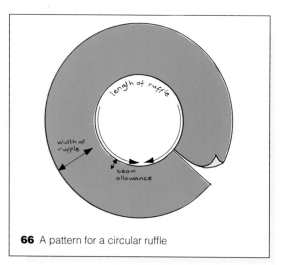

**66** A pattern for a circular ruffle

make a paper pattern first. Draw a circle the circumference of which is the *length* you want the finished ruffle to be. Draw an outer circle, the *width* you want the finished ruffle away from the first circle, plus turnings. Cut across the circle, snip the inside seam allowance and open out the ruffle.

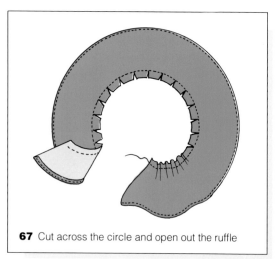

**67** Cut across the circle and open out the ruffle

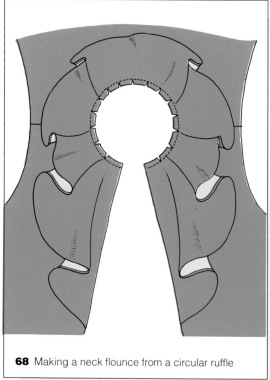

**68** Making a neck flounce from a circular ruffle

A circular ruffle can be extended to form a neck flounce by joining several spirals together. Make the joins coincide with the shoulder seams. The spiral can be shaped to widen out at the centre front to form a jabot.

# ATTACHING CIRCULAR RUFFLES

First, neaten the outer edge of the ruffle as for a straight frill. The waterfall frill added at the neckline is positioned right side up and stitched in with a seam to give the desired effect. A waterfall frill falling from a cuff would be inserted between the cuff edges with the right side to the top cuff, so that it falls correctly.

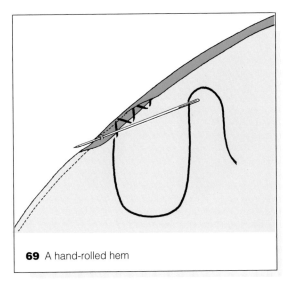

**69** A hand-rolled hem

Straight frills require a gathering thread along the unfinished edge. For long frills, divide the strip into sections and gather each section separately.

### ▶ A STRAIGHT RUFFLE

A straight ruffle is made from a continuous strip of fabric usually cut on the straight grain. Fabric which is almost the same on both sides is suitable. First decide on the *width* you want, add turnings and allow approximately three times the amount of fabric for the *length* of the strip. The length you need will depend on how full you want the ruffle to be and the type of fabric. Fine fabric will take a fuller ruffle.

Neaten one long edge of the strip with a hand-rolled hem (see fig. 69 above) or a narrow hem using the relevant attachment on your machine. Narrow hemming on an overlock machine gives a superb finish to the edge of the frill (see p. 109).

Gather up the raw edge of the frill using a row of small running stitches to fit the edge to which it is to be attached. Insert the frill between the front edge and the facing band before these are stitched together.

# THE COLLAR

The trickiest part of making up a collar is not attaching it to the neckline but making a good collar edge. The edges play a large part in achieving a professional, flat, well-shaped and even finish to a blouse. A good deal of work also goes into making them lie correctly.

Interface the under part of the collar and tack the collar pieces right sides together, stitching exactly on the marked line. Trim away *all* the interfacing in the seam line. Trim the seam line down to 6 mm ($\frac{1}{4}$ in) or *less*. With thick fabric, layer the seams – that is, trim

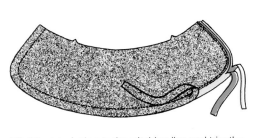

**70** Trim interfacing to the stitching line and trim the seam turnings

down one seam a little more than the other. This prevents a ridge.

Cut small notches out of a collar curve and clip *almost all* the seam turning away at the collar point.

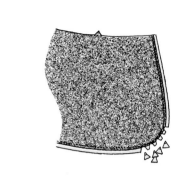

**71** Cut away as much fabric as you can at the corner of a collar

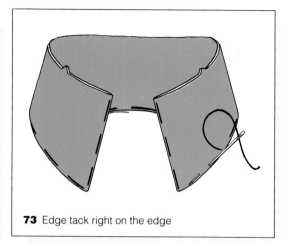

**73** Edge tack right on the edge

**72** Cut away excess fabric to give a sharper collar point

## ATTACHING COLLARS WITHOUT ADDITIONAL BLOUSE FACINGS

A standing collar, a band collar and a fairly straight roll collar are often attached without the addition of a facing to neaten the neck edge. It is an easy way to attach a collar because the collar facing (the under collar) itself, is used to neaten the raw edge. This involves an extra stage in the making up of the collar.

Turn the collar right side out. Work the seam line between the finger and thumb so that the seam is exactly on the edge. Hold the seam by working a line of small tacking stitches right on the edge.

Press the collar first on the right side and then the underside. When the blouse is finished remove the edge tacking and press lightly along the edge to take out any imprint of the tacking.

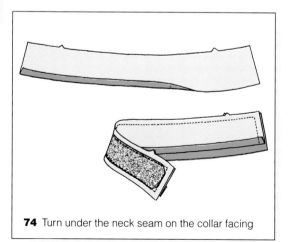

**74** Turn under the neck seam on the collar facing

Turn under the neck seam allowance of the collar facing along the stitching line before stitching the outside collar edges. Make up the collar as in fig. 74 on previous page. Clip the neck curves and straighten the neck edge.

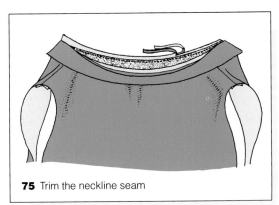

**75** Trim the neckline seam

Match the notches and shoulder marks and place the collar to the neck edge. Tack and stitch along the seam line. Trim the seam to 6 mm ($\frac{1}{4}$ in). If this is the interfaced side, trim all the interfacing from the seam line.

Bring the folded edge to lie on the stitching line, enclosing the turnings and hand hem. If you've made a standing or band collar you will find attaching a shirt collar with a band

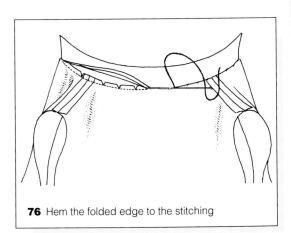

**76** Hem the folded edge to the stitching

easy to understand. The procedure is the same, but the two halves of the band are added separately and the collar is sandwiched between the two.

# ATTACHING A SHIRT COLLAR WITH A BAND

Complete the collar as fig. 76, plus any top-stitching.

With right sides together, interface and attach the first side of the band. Trim and clip the seam.

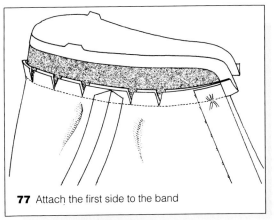

**77** Attach the first side to the band

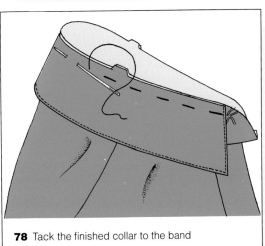

**78** Tack the finished collar to the band

Tack the finished collar to the collar band, taking particular care to match the centre-front line and all the markings and notches. Turn under the seam allowance on the neck edge of the other band piece (the band facing) as fig. 78 on p. 73 and tack. With right sides together, tack this band over the collar and stitch this curve taking care to follow the stitching lines exactly at the centre-fronts.

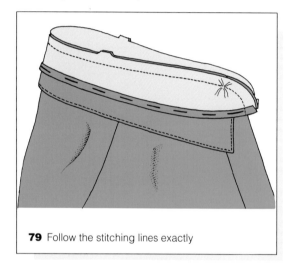

**79** Follow the stitching lines exactly

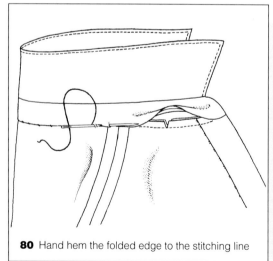

**80** Hand hem the folded edge to the stitching line

Trim the seam as before and clip the curves. Bring the folded edge over to lie on the stitching line and hand hem it in place.

## ATTACHING COLLARS BY MEANS OF A FACING

A curved roll collar is attached by means of a facing. It is still sandwiched between two layers of fabric, but in this case it lies between the blouse and an additional facing. This facing can be an extended facing – that is, forming part of the blouse front and folded back on itself – or, it can be a separate piece of material which is stitched to the blouse front – which means there will be a seam on the front edge of the blouse.

Make up the collar as before. It is very important to keep all the dots and notches clearly marked, as this type of collar stops short of the edge of the facing. Mark all the dots accurately and you will have no problem with aligning the collar edge. Complete the facing with the correct type of interfacing (see p. 44). Make up the collar as in fig. 73.

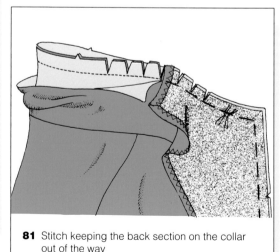

**81** Stitch keeping the back section on the collar out of the way

Place the collar to the neck edge, matching the notches, and tack in place. Fold the facing right sides inside, over the collar. Snip the seam allowance of the collar at the point where the facing ends at each side. Keeping this section of the collar out of the way, stitch along the neck edge.

Trim the seams and corners and turn the facing to the inside. Turn under the seam allowance on the free edge of the collar and hem it down on to the stitching line.

If there is a back neck facing included in the pattern, first join the shoulder seams of the facing and the back neck facing. Press

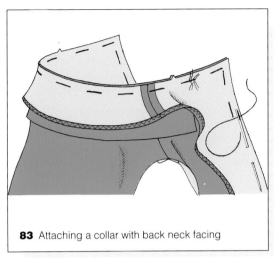

**83** Attaching a collar with back neck facing

them open. Open out the neck curve and the facing, folding them right sides together and sandwich the collar in between. Make sure that the centre lines and the notches match. Tack and stitch.

Trim the neckline seam and cut off the corners and turn the facing to the inside and press.

A *flat* collar is also attached with a complete facing. Complete the collar. Join the facings at the shoulder seams and press them open.

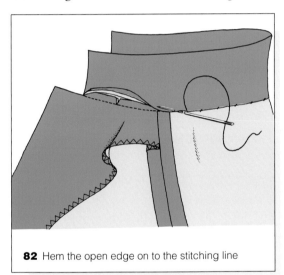

**82** Hem the open edge on to the stitching line

Neaten the outer edge of the facing with a small zigzag stitch. Tack the collar to the neck edge taking care that all the notches and marks are matched. Tack the facing, wrong side uppermost, over the collar and stitch the neck curve exactly on the stitching line. Trim the seam to 6 mm ($\frac{1}{4}$ in) and clip the curve.

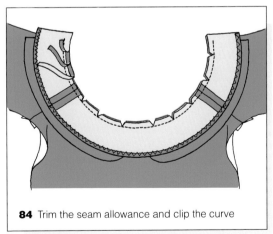

**84** Trim the seam allowance and clip the curve

Turn the facing to the inside. A flat collar will lie better if it is *understitched*. Press the facing and the seam turnings away from the collar. Machine stitch close to the collar edge

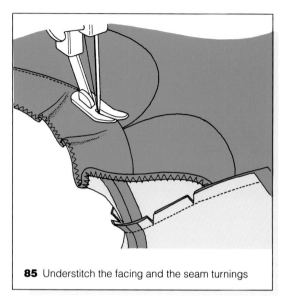

**85** Understitch the facing and the seam turnings

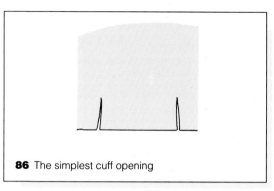

**86** The simplest cuff opening

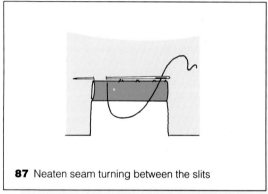

**87** Neaten seam turning between the slits

through the thicknesses of the seam turnings and facing together.

When using a thick fabric, a collar can be attached in two separate halves. The under collar is attached to the garment and the upper collar to the facing. This is sometimes called a notched collar (see jacket collar p. 97). A shawl collar is also attached in two separate halves.

# CUFFS

You do not have to stick with the cuff opening suggested in your pattern. With blouses where the designer has made a feature of the opening, you will obviously want to keep to the pattern, e.g. a shirt-cuff opening which is turned to the right side and top-stitched. But in most cases you can choose to do a very simple opening.

## ▶ A SIMPLE CUFF OPENING

The simplest opening is made with two slits cut into the seam allowance about 3.5 cm ($1\frac{1}{2}$ in) apart. The seam turning between the slits is neatened and turned to the inside. Where the cuff overlaps the opening is folded back on itself.

## ▶ FACED SLIT CUFF OPENING

The faced slit opening is another quick and simple cuff opening. Mark the position of the cuff opening. Cut a strip of fabric the length of the opening, plus 2.5 cm (1 in) and about 6 cm ($2\frac{1}{2}$ in) wide. Neaten the edges and place this facing over the marked line, right sides together.

Stitch each side of the line, tapering to a fine point at the end. Slash the opening almost to the stitches at the end. Turn the facing to the wrong side, work the seam line to the edge and press.

**88** Stitch each side of the line to a fine point and cut

**89** Turn the facing to the wrong side and work seam line to edge

The difference between these two openings is that whereas the edges of a faced opening meet, the edges of the bound opening and the shirt opening overlap, and this should be taken into account when choosing the type of opening in relation to the cuff. With a

faced opening the cuff itself must project beyond the facing edge to overlap. With the other openings, the cuff edges are in line with the overlapping edges of the opening.

### ▶ A BOUND OPENING

Reinforce the slash line for the opening with a line of stitching each side of the line. Slash

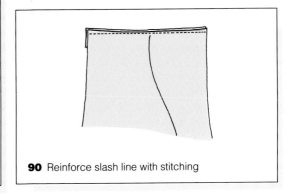

**90** Reinforce slash line with stitching

the opening and straighten it out. Cut a strip of fabric 3 cm ($1\frac{1}{4}$ in) wide and the full length of the slash. Press under 6 mm ($\frac{1}{4}$ in) on the long side. Place the raw edge of the strip to the edge of the opening, right sides together and stitch, sleeve side uppermost. Bring the folded edge over on the line of stitching and

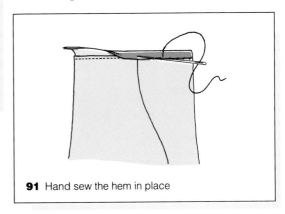

**91** Hand sew the hem in place

hand sew the hem in place. Fold the binding in half and turn the front edge to the wrong side of the sleeve and press.

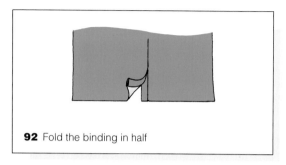

**92** Fold the binding in half

## ATTACHING THE CUFF

A cuff can be cut in one piece and folded back on itself or cut in two separate halves – a cuff and a cuff facing. Interface one side of the cuff only. For a one-piece cuff, interface only half of the cuff, catch stitching the interfacing to the fold line.

Turn under the seam turning on the cuff facing and trim it to 6 mm ($\frac{1}{4}$ in). With right sides together, tack the facing to the cuff and stitch across the ends.

Trim the interfacing from the seam line, trim down and layer the seam and cut off the corners, turn and press, as for the collar (see p. 71).

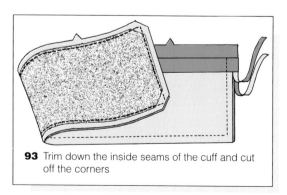

**93** Trim down the inside seams of the cuff and cut off the corners

With right sides together, pin the cuff to the sleeve edge, keeping the cuff facing pinned out of the way. It is easier to accommodate the fullness in the sleeve if you work from the inside of the sleeve and insert the pins vertically.

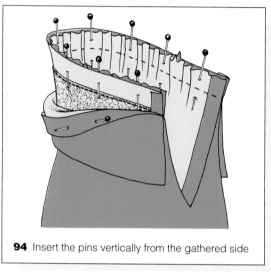

**94** Insert the pins vertically from the gathered side

Tack and stitch, using the free-arm on your machine with the gathered side uppermost. Trim the seam to 6 mm ($\frac{1}{4}$ in). Bring the fold of the facing down to the stitching line and hand sew the hem in place. Cuffs are vastly improved with top-stitching.

# SETTING IN A SLEEVE

Sleeves are no longer the bogey to the home dressmaker that they once were. Tightly fitting armholes and rigid shoulder lines have been replaced with an easier fit and more versatile shapes.

If you keep to the basic principles of good home dressmaking – follow your pattern accurately by marking everything you possibly can – sleeves present no problem. Even a set-in sleeve with a smooth sleeve head is simplified by marking the stitching lines and putting them together *exactly* where the designer intended. It is when you become a bit careless about the seam turnings – a little less in the sleeve head, a little more off the shoulder line – that it becomes difficult to fit the two together.

The shirt sleeve with an extended shoulder line has become no more difficult than stitching a flat seam. The shoulder seam is joined before the underarm seams as the pieces have no built-in shaping and are joined flat. The seam can be top-stitched.

### ► A SET-IN SLEEVE

A set-in sleeve may have a gathered sleeve head or a smooth sleeve head. The difference is that with the smooth sleeve head the fabric is eased into a rounded shape and with the gathered sleeve head the fullness is distributed into even gathers. However, the method for inserting them is the same.

First, mark the stitching line of the armhole on the bodice and on the sleeve (on a multi-sized pattern measure in the seam allowance 1.5 cm ($\frac{5}{8}$ in) from the cut edge). Mark the dot indicating the top of the sleeve and make sure that you have clear notches, back and front. Join the underarm sleeve seam and

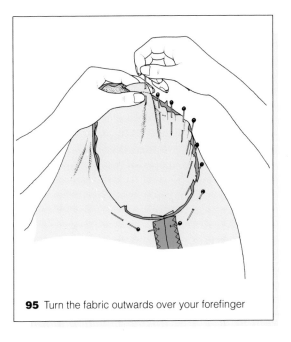

**95** Turn the fabric outwards over your forefinger

press it open. Check that you have two facing sleeves – a right and a left.

Work a row of very tiny gathering stitches by hand from the single notch to the double notch round the head of the sleeve, *just inside* the stitching line on the seam turning. Ease up the fabric along this thread, just a little.

With the blouse and sleeve right side out, insert the sleeve into the armhole and work

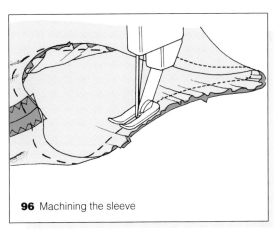

**96** Machining the sleeve

from the inside looking into the sleeve. Pin the underarm, between the notches. Next, pin the mark at the sleeve head to the shoulder line. Now work down from the top, turning the fabric outwards over your forefinger in small sections, to the first notch, placing the pins vertically. Go back to the top and work down the other side. Tack with a small running stitch on the stitching line.

For a gathered sleeve head, spread out the gathers and look at them horizontally to check that the fabric is in even flutes.

Even if your machine has a sleeve arm, it is better to stitch the sleeve gathered side uppermost so that you can check to see if the fullness is puckering as you stitch.

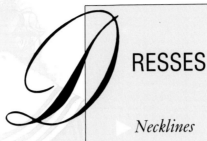

## CHAPTER EIGHT

# Dresses

> *Necklines*

> *Pockets for dresses*

> *Setting in a dress zip*

> *Putting in shoulder pads*

> *Buttonholes on a dress*

The dress section is probably one of the most tempting and exciting parts of the pattern catalogue. This is probably because a dress is one of the most difficult items to buy off-the-peg in a style and colour that will suit you. There are so many elements to consider; the length, neckline, sleeves, waistline, and of course the line and silhouette you want to achieve.

Making a dress gives you the opportunity to try out new fabrics and exciting new patterns with a wide variety of neckline shapes. There are draped necklines, cut low at the back, high cowl necks, faced necklines of all shapes, cross over bodices, sailor and shawl collars as well as the traditional collar types.

Because you are working on the whole silhouette, a dress can transform your figure. An ankle length dress with a flowing line in a plain fabric and bold colour will look and make you feel quite different from an above-the-knee tailored coat dress in a two-colour check or contrasting stripe. This chapter has information on shoulder pads which transform a silhouette by creating height and giving an impression of slimness. Experiment with various sizes and shapes of shoulder pads until you get the look you want.

But it isn't just the length and fullness of the skirt which you have to take into account, the neckline of the dress can also alter your appearance. A V-neck slims the face and elongates the neck while a round high neck has the opposite effect, particularly if it is collarless. By making a dress for yourself you can experiment with the boldest of fabric designs in a style which you know will suit *you*.

# NECKLINES
## FACED NECKLINES

Shaped necklines, which are neatened with a facing turned to the inside, are the simplest type of neckline. The facing itself should be interfaced with a lightweight interfacing. An iron-on type is suitable for small areas like this. Too stiff an interfacing will make the neck stand away from the body.

It is easy to substitute a faced neckline for a collar in a pattern, should you want to, by cutting a facing following the shape of the neck edge of the pattern.

### ► TO CUT A NECK FACING FROM A PATTERN

Use tracing paper or transparent lightweight interfacing to make the pattern. Trace the neck edge, front and shoulder of the pattern piece and cut it out. Following the neck curve, draw a line 6.5 cm ($2\frac{1}{2}$ in) away from it. Mark the grain line in the same direction as the body pattern piece and cut out the facing pattern. Cut the front and back neck facing in this way.

Interface the front and back facing, join them at the shoulders and cut away the interfacing from the seam line. Neaten the outer curved edge, preferably with a small zigzag, as turning in a small hem at the edge may show as a ridge on the right side in some fabrics.

With right sides together, match the side seams and tack. Stitch the facing to the neck edge. If there is a zip, wrap the ends of the facing around the open edge of the back zip.

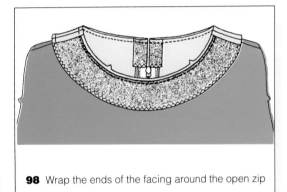

**98** Wrap the ends of the facing around the open zip

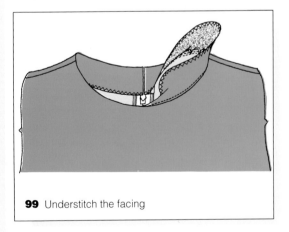

**99** Understitch the facing

**97** To cut a neck facing from a pattern

Trim the seam and clip the curve. *Under-stitch the facing* – that is, turn the facing away from the dress and stitch through the facing and the seam turnings together. This prevents the facing from rolling up and showing on the right side.

Stitch the facing to the shoulder seams only. Hem the ends of the facing to the zip tape.

# A CRAVAT OR NECK BOW

It is quite simple to add a soft, tie collar or to substitute a large floppy bow or cravat for an existing collar on any dress pattern which has a round neckline. Finish the front neck opening first.

### ▶ MAKING A PATTERN FOR A CRAVAT OR NECK BOW

First determine the length you want the tie. For a tie long enough to go round the neck, leaving ends long enough to make into a good bow, this will be a full length of approximately 132 cm (60 in). Cut a pattern for the tie in tissue paper or a *very* lightweight interfacing. Interfacing is ideal as it can be tacked on to the neck to try it out and re-shaped in any way you like. The actual cravat or bow is not interfaced.

Cut the pattern to half the required length, as it will be cut out from double fabric. Make the width of the tie between 12.5 cm (5 in) and 20 cm (8 in), depending on whether you want to fold the tie over at the neck (which will form a soft collar) and on the width you want the finished bow. Mark the grain line on the pattern at 45 degrees to the straight edge.

Try out the pattern. Fold it in half length-wise and pin one edge to the neck edge from the centre-back neck of the dress along one side of the neck to the centre-front. You can

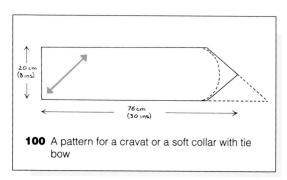

**100** A pattern for a cravat or a soft collar with tie bow

then shape the ends in any way you like and also narrow the width at the neck edge, if necessary. Remember to allow for turnings.

When you are happy with the shape, cut out the pattern on double fabric and on the cross, as indicated by the grain line.

Stitch the short ends at the centre-back and press the seam open. Stay-stitch the neck edge (see p. 40) and clip the seam turnings almost to the stitching. With the right sides together, tack the tie to the neck edge and stitch.

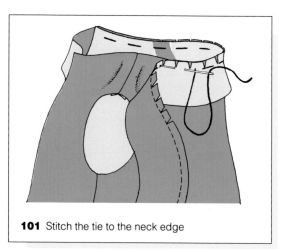

**101** Stitch the tie to the neck edge

Fold the tie right sides together, stitch across the ends and along the length of the rest of the tie. Trim the seams.

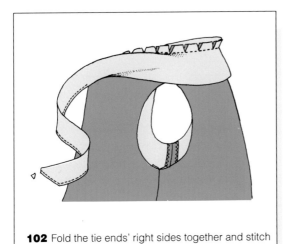

**102** Fold the tie ends' right sides together and stitch

Turn the ends of the tie right side out. Edge-tack and press the tie. Turn under the seam allowance on the remaining raw edge of the tie and hem the fold down on the stitching line.

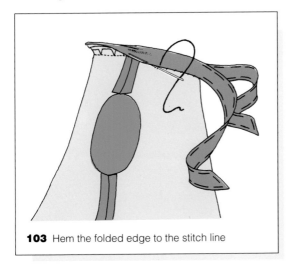

**103** Hem the folded edge to the stitch line

# POCKETS

## DECORATIVE POCKETS

As with a skirt, pockets can be set into the side seam of any dress, whether the pattern provides them or not; but with a dress, pockets are often made into a design feature.

## PATCH POCKETS

Patch pockets are made up first and placed on top of the dress. It is always easier to stitch them on before stitching up the body seams of the dress. However, they are more often decorative than functional and if you have altered the dress pattern in any way, pin the pocket in position and look at it in a mirror and use your judgement to find the most balanced position.

Patch pockets are almost always improved by the addition of a very lightweight interfacing, even if this is not indicated in the pattern. Sheer iron-on interfacing is suitable for this small area unless the fabric dictates otherwise. Pocket flaps and welts should always be interfaced.

An unlined patch pocket is the simplest, but it needs exact cutting and stitching to get a professional look. Interface the pocket with

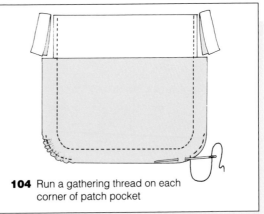

**104** Run a gathering thread on each corner of patch pocket

extra-lightweight interfacing, to the fold line. Neaten the top pocket edge with a small zig-zag stitch or narrow hem. Turn the edge of the pocket to the outside along the fold line and stitch the ends. Continue the stitching line round the outer edge of the pocket, just outside the seam line, to mark the fold line.

Trim the seam and turn the hem to the wrong side. Press. Run a gathering thread, by hand, round each corner. Ease up the fullness and turn the seam allowance to the inside. Tack and press. Edge stitch the pocket to the dress.

# POCKET FLAPS

A pocket flap can be added to any patch pocket, cutting it to the same width, plus turnings and to a third or quarter of its depth, depending on the size of the pocket. Interface the flap, place right sides together and stitch, leaving open the top edge. Stitch the top corners obliquely, as shown.

Trim the inside edges, turn the pocket flap and stitch it in place. First stitch the edge of the seam turnings just below the line marked on the dress, then turn the flap downwards and stitch the right side of the flap along the fold line.

Top-stitching should be completed before the pockets or flaps are attached to the dress. It is easier to top-stitch the pocket edges and actually attach the pocket to the dress with invisible hand sewing from the inside of the dress.

A square patch pocket is made in the same way, and the best way to get neat corners is to mitre them. It doesn't take a moment and it is well worth the extra work. Mark the seam allowance, by continuing the stitching right round the pocket as above and then press the seam turnings to the inside. Open the turnings out at each corner, turn in the fabric diagonally at the corner and press. Fold this creased line in half, right sides together. Stitch by hand using a small running stitch on the creased line.

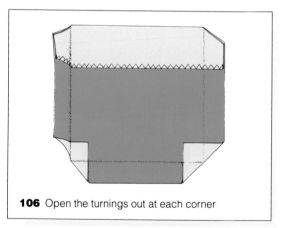

**106** Open the turnings out at each corner

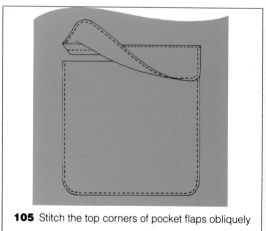

**105** Stitch the top corners of pocket flaps obliquely

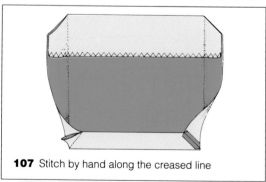

**107** Stitch by hand along the creased line

Trim the seam and turn it to the inside. Re-press the corner.

# A DRESS ZIP

### ▶ A BACK ZIP

If your dress has a back zip the easiest time to put it in is once the back seam has been joined, but before the side seams are joined, so that the fabric can be placed flat on the table.

The zip in a skirt is usually inserted into a curved seam, under the right hand seam turning which laps over and completely conceals it. It is stitched a little away from the seam line as the seam tends to open against the curve of the hip. A back dress zip, however, is inserted into a flat seam. It can be put in by the same method, but as the fabric lies flatter, it can also be put in as a centred zip.

### ▶ A CENTRED ZIP

Tack up the zip opening using a small running stitch. Press the seam open. Lay the fabric flat, right side down and place the zip, face down, with the teeth centred over the seam line and the zip pull 6 mm ($\frac{1}{4}$ in) down from the neck seam line. Tack in position.

On the right side, use a seam guide and a coloured thread to mark an accurate line to follow, for top-stitching the zip 7 mm ($\frac{3}{8}$ in) away from the seam, tapering to a point at the base. If the back neck facing has already been attached, fold it away from the neck edge.

Top-stitch the zip in a matching thread. On delicate fabric, use a tiny, almost invisible half backstitch to top-stitch the zip by hand (see p. 40). Remove the tacking holding the seam edges together.

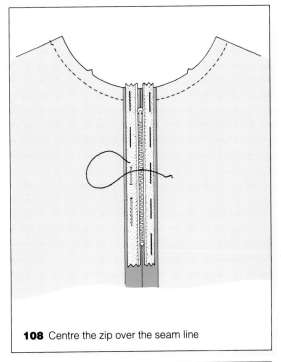

**108** Centre the zip over the seam line

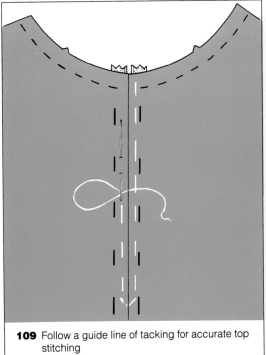

**109** Follow a guide line of tacking for accurate top stitching

Fold the facing to the inside, turn under the raw edges and hem them to the zip tape. Sew a small hook and eye at the neck edge.

## WAISTLINES

Joining a skirt and bodice at the waist is not difficult, but with a very full skirt it can be awkward because of the amount of fullness involved.

Work a row of tiny gathering stitches round the waist or at those areas to be gathered, just outside the stitching line, using a buttonhole twist. This is an extra thick thread for working hand buttonholes and will be strong enough to support the weight of the fabric.

With the skirt wrong side out and the bodice right side out, drop the bodice inside the skirt so that the right sides are facing. Match the centre front and back seams, darts and notches. Pin these, inserting the pins

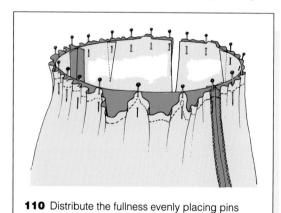

**110** Distribute the fullness evenly placing pins vertically

vertically. Draw up the fullness in sections, distributing the fullness evenly.

To check the evenness of the gathering, hold the fabric almost at eye level and look at the gathers horizontally. They should be in even flutes with no flat spaces. Stitch the waistline seam with the gathers uppermost.

# SHOULDER PADS

Shoulder pads can change the look of a dress completely. They not only give shape and structure but, unbelievably, they are slimming! Try it for yourself. Look at your dress in front of a full length mirror without the pads, then slip in a medium-sized pad, inserting the thick edge into the sleeve head as far as the edge of the seam turning. By adding height, the overall look is longer and leaner and by adding bulk the bust is made to look that bit smaller.

Shoulder pads now come in all shapes and sizes and it is important to choose the best size for the look you want to achieve. Set-in sleeves need pads with the thickness of the pad at the edge of the shoulder. Raglan sleeves with dropped or extended shoulder lines, need pads which are curved to the shape of the shoulder, with the thickness of the pad on top. The thickness of the pads you use is a matter of preference. They can be bought in small, medium and large.

Sleeves which are very gathered over the sleeve head may need additional support in some fabrics, to make the gathers stand up. A narrow, boat-shaped pad called a sleeve puff is designed for this.

Shoulder pads should be covered either in the dress fabric or in a matching lining. Cut a piece of fabric twice the size of the pad. Centre it on the fabric and fold the fabric over it, thereby encasing the pad. Smooth the fabric to the contours of the pad without flattening the thickness, then trim the fabric to the size of the pad. Tack and zigzag stitch through all the thicknesses. For a very shaped pad, make a dart or a seam at the centre of the pad so that the fabric takes its shape. Stretch fabric, especially nylon tights the colour of the dress, are ideal for covering shoulder pads.

### ▶ INSERTING A SHOULDER PAD INTO A SET-IN SLEEVE

Place the centre of the thick edge of the pad to the shoulder seam, allowing it to extend to the edge of the seam turnings. (Remember, the dress is inside out and so the curve of the pad is the wrong way up, i.e. concave.) Stitch the pad to the seam turnings, using a small

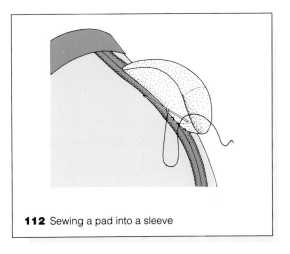

**112** Sewing a pad into a sleeve

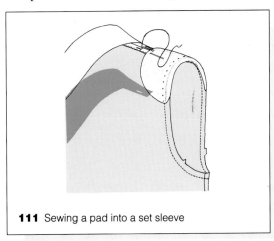

**111** Sewing a pad into a set sleeve

stab stitch through all thicknesses without flattening the edge of the pad. At the opposite edge of the pad, make several loose stitches about 1 cm ($\frac{1}{2}$ in) long to attach the pad to the shoulder seam.

### ▶ INSERTING A PAD INTO A RAGLAN SLEEVE

Try on the dress to find the best position for the pad and pin the pad to hold it in place. Turn the dress wrong side out and slip stitch the pad along the shoulder seam to hold it.

### ▶ INSERTING A SLEEVE PUFF

A sleeve puff is stitched to the armhole seam with the pad projecting into the sleeve head. If you find that pads on evening dresses with draped or wide necklines do not stay in place, anchor the dress with lingerie ribbon guards.

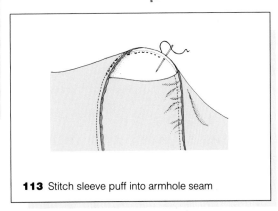

**113** Stitch sleeve puff into armhole seam

# BUTTONHOLES

Most dressmakers sew buttonholes by machine; follow the instructions in your machine manual for this. On very fine silk or polyester jersey, you may prefer to sew buttonholes by hand. Whichever way you choose, mark them accurately and the starting point for this is the centre-front line.

The length of the buttonhole is the diameter of the button plus 3 mm ($\frac{1}{8}$ in). Very domed buttons may need a little more than this. As a general guide, horizontal buttonholes have a quarter of this measurement outside the centre-front line (that is, nearer the front edge) and three quarters to the inside. Mark the ends of the buttonholes with two lines of tacking, parallel to the centre-front, and stitch the position for the buttonhole between the lines following your pattern.

Vertical buttonholes and buttons are stitched *on* the centre front line. They are worked in the same way as horizontal buttonholes but have a bar at each end.

Buttonholes should always be worked on interfaced fabric. In lightweight and jersey fabric, use the sheerest interfacing.

Slit the buttonhole on the marked line and work round the edge with tiny oversewing stitches in fine thread, to hold the cut edges together and prevent stretching.

Secure the thread at the back of the work and bring out the needle at the edge of the slit at the inner left hand edge of the buttonhole. Work from left to right so that you don't cover the stitches as you progress. Insert the needle from underneath and bring it out *not more* than 3 mm ($\frac{1}{8}$ in) from the edge of the slit, and preferably less. Bring the double end of the thread round and under the point of the needle, to form a knot on the cut edge. Work along the edge, keeping the stitches uniform and vertical.

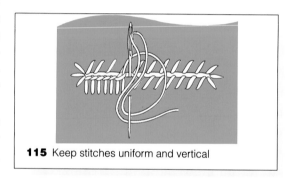

**115** Keep stitches uniform and vertical

Fan out the stitches at the end, taking 5–7 stitches, and work along the second side. Work a bar tack across the end. Take four long stitches in the same place across the width of the two rows of buttonhole stitches. Insert the needle at one end, under the thread bar, but over the needle thread. Work along the bar, easing the stitches very close together.

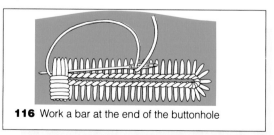

**116** Work a bar at the end of the buttonhole

**114** Work the oversewing stitches in fine thread to hold the cut edges together

90

## CHAPTER NINE

# ACKETS

*Interfacing for jackets*

*Jacket pockets*

*Attaching a collar*

*Making jacket sleeves*

*Lining a jacket*

ailoring is a technique where you build a permanent shape into a garment, with expert sewing techniques, steaming and pressing. This is done with specialised equipment and heavy irons and it is not possible to produce the same result at home (home tailoring is 'soft' tailoring). But what you can do, is to refine your own dressmaking skills to such an extent that you can make a passable imitation of it and produce a jacket with sharp clean lines which is moulded to your figure and will keep its shape.

Tailoring techniques require attention to detail, so the seams will need to be flat and well pressed, all the edges trimmed turned and pressed to a fine edge and any top stitching will be precise. It is details like this and, in particular, the top stitching and the choice of buttons, which will make all the difference to the finished jacket.

In a wool jersey, velour or any pile fabric, top stitching with a single line of a regular machine stitch, using a matching thread, is all that is needed to give definition to the jacket edges. But in a smooth cloth, such as a worsted or gaberdine, experiment with different ways of top stitching. Try a very narrow satin stitch about 2 mm ($\frac{1}{8}$ in) wide using a thread which is one shade lighter or darker than the fabric and worked about 1 cm ($\frac{1}{2}$ in) in from the edge of the front and collar edges. This can often look as though the stitching has been woven into the fabric and not added later.

Making a lined jacket is possibly one of the most difficult garments you will attempt as a home dressmaker, so work your way towards it gradually by perfecting your skills in buttonholing, top stitching, and setting-in sleeves and collars. If you fit your pattern as you have learned with all your other garments, you will find making a tailored jacket very satisfying.

Because the fabric is shaped by pressing, the best choice for your first attempt at tailoring is wool. Choose a firmly woven, medium to heavyweight wool.

# THE INTERFACING

The interfacing used in tailoring is canvas. It comes in a range of weights.

- Hair canvas is ideal as this has a percentage of goat's hair mixed with it which makes it springy and helps it keep its shape without creasing.
- Use a softer canvas for small areas and for lighter weight wools and heavy linen.
- Collar linen is a very firm canvas for under collars. It is woven with warp and weft threads of equal weight.

Canvas is available in iron-on form also, but to begin with, use sew-in hair canvas throughout for your coat or jacket, so that you learn the basic hand stitches involved in tailoring. Later on you may want to try out the other types of canvas.

Hair canvas has a grain and the pieces must be cut following the straight grain of the pattern pieces given.

Use a tracing wheel and dressmaker's carbon to transfer the markings from the pattern to the canvas. Use tailor's tacking to thread mark the fabric. Make a bold line of tacking in contrasting thread for the centre-front and back.

Interfacing in tailoring is applied to the wrong side of the jacket fabric and not to the facing. Any darts are slashed and overlapped at the stitching line. It's best to deal with the pockets first.

# WELT AND FLAP POCKETS

A welt pocket is used quite often on a tailored jacket. It is decorative and stylish and not easy! It is, of course, just a combination of a pocket flap and a bound buttonhole, but they must both be sewn with precision. The flap and the bound slit must both be the correct size and there is no margin for error!

Flap pockets are made in exactly the same way as welt pockets, but the flap is attached to the top stitching line of the bound slit of the pocket opening, and hangs over the top to conceal it. A welt is stitched to the bottom stitching line of the opening and folds upwards to conceal the slit.

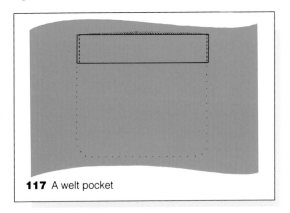

**117** A welt pocket

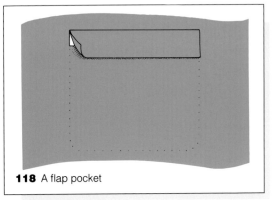

**118** A flap pocket

Once again, mark everything! Accurately! And then mark the outline of the pocket exactly with a line of tacking thread. In fabric which frays, loosely woven or fine fabric, reinforce the pocket area on the inside of the fabric with a very lightweight iron-on interfacing.

Complete the pocket welt first. Interface one side of the welt (trim the seam allowance from the interfacing) and stitch the ends. Cut off the corners and trim the seam turnings.

Turn the welt right side out, edge tack and press. Tack the open edge of the welt along the stitching line and cut off the corners. If the welt or flap is to be top-stitched, this must be done at this stage.

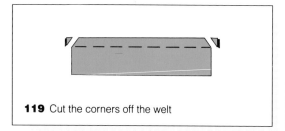

**119** Cut the corners off the welt

Tack the welt to the right side of the jacket, matching the stitching line of the welt to the stitching line of the pocket marked on the jacket exactly.

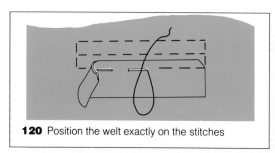

**120** Position the welt exactly on the stitches

Pin the pocket piece over the welt on the right side of the jacket. (The pocket section may be one long piece, which folds in half to form the pocket bag, or cut as two separate pieces.) Tack the pocket over the welt on the marked stitching lines. Working from the wrong side of the jacket, stitch the rectangle for the pocket, making accurate corners and taking care not to extend the stitching lines beyond the edge of the welt at the corners.

Slash the pocket along the cutting line, stopping short of the corners. Cut diagonally to the stitching line in the corners. You will find it easier to slash the pocket line and jacket line separately.

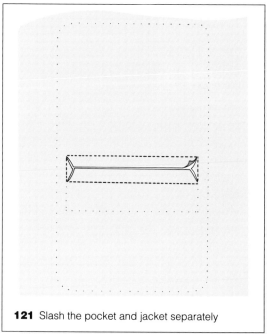

**121** Slash the pocket and jacket separately

Turn the pocket through the opening to the wrong side and press it. Fold the pocket piece with the right sides together. Stitch round the outside edge, catching in the tiny triangular sections at each end of the slash.

On the right side of the jacket, fold the welt upwards and stitch the ends, by hand or by machine.

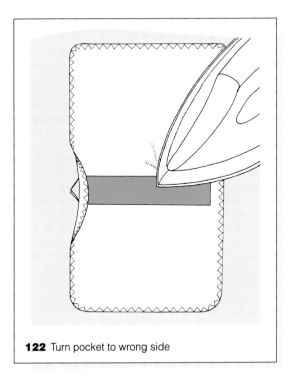

**122** Turn pocket to wrong side

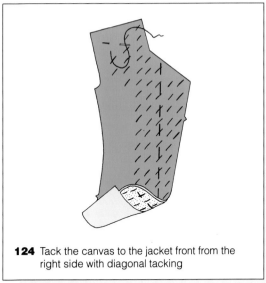

**124** Tack the canvas to the jacket front from the right side with diagonal tacking

fabric right side up and 'flash baste' (long diagonal tacking) from the right side.

Turn the jacket to the wrong side and stitch the inside edge of the interfacing to the front using a loose catch stitch (see p. 41). Since this is a permanent stitch, take up only a thread from the fabric, so that the stitch is not visible from the right side.

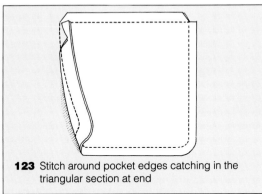

**123** Stitch around pocket edges catching in the triangular section at end

# INTERFACING THE JACKET

### ▶ THE JACKET FRONT

The jacket must be kept flat and smooth on the table as you work. Position the interfacing to the front edge of the jacket and pin the centre-front lines together. Turn the jacket

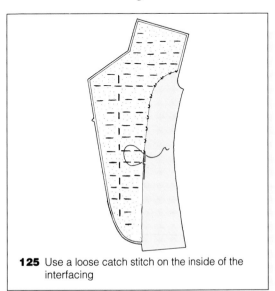

**125** Use a loose catch stitch on the inside of the interfacing

### ▶ THE JACKET BACK

This is also interfaced across the shoulders. Flash baste the interfacing to the jacket back as before and loosely catch stitch the edge.

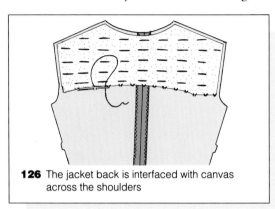

**126** The jacket back is interfaced with canvas across the shoulders

Join the front and back jacket at the shoulder seams. Cut away *all* the canvas from the shoulder seam turnings and press the seams open.

### ▶ THE COLLAR

The under collar is attached next and this is usually cut in two halves placed on the cross grain. Cut the canvas interfacing for the collar in the same way. Stitch the seams in the fabric under collar and press it open. Lap the seams in the canvas under collar and stitch a flat seam.

Place the canvas collar to the wrong side of the under collar. Keeping them flat on the table, tack them together round the outside edges on the stitching line.

If a roll or crease line is marked on the under collar, work a running stitch in matching thread along this line. If no roll line is marked, estimate it by fitting the collar to your back neck. The roll line is the division between the stand and fall of the collar.

The canvas is fused to the collar with pad

stitching. This is a small diagonal tacking worked in parallel lines with stitches approximately 1 cm ($\frac{3}{8}$ in) long. Having finished one line of stitches do not reverse the work but stitch in the opposite direction. The stitches are staggered so that the canvas is not drawn up into tucks.

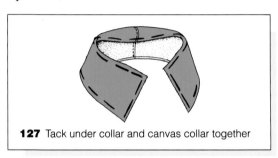

**127** Tack under collar and canvas collar together

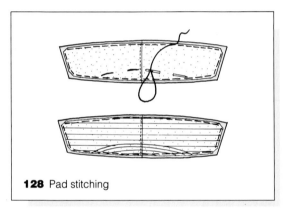

**128** Pad stitching

Pad stitch the curve of the stand of the collar first. To help you get the curve right it is a good idea to pencil lines on the canvas as a guide. The pad stitching on the fall is done in straight lines and it is useful to also pencil these in at the same time.

Hold the collar with the stand towards you and the canvas side uppermost and work the rows of pad-stitching, following the curve of the stand, over your forefinger. Do not take the stitching into the seam turnings.

Pad stitch the fall of the collar keeping it

# Formal Wear

Both work and social occasions require formal outfits. Suits, tailored dresses and separates are all ideal for both formal parties and the office. Use colour and design to create your own special look.

## The Dress

If you're planning a wedding you'll know how much thought goes into the bride's dress – it is *the* dress everyone will be looking at! And if you're *not* planning a wedding don't pass the wedding dresses by – because they make fabulous ball gowns.

## Casual Wear

Casual wear should be comfortable, whatever occasion it's for. Casual clothes cover everything from beach wear to your favourite dinner party outfit; shorts, shirts, dresses, leggings and casual jackets. Create your own style!

# Evening Wear

Even if you don't go to a ball every month it's wonderful to have a party dress in your wardrobe. Use beautiful fabrics to make the most of exciting and sophisticated designs.

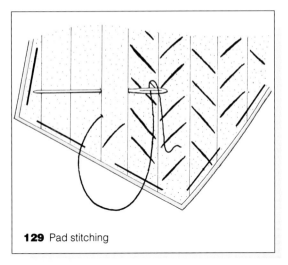

**129** Pad stitching

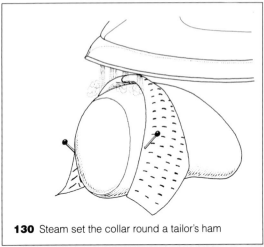

**130** Steam set the collar round a tailor's ham

flat. Then trim away all the canvas in the seam allowance right round the collar edge.

Fold the under collar along the roll line. Then, using a steam iron and a damp cloth, steam the fall of the collar. Pull the outer edge slightly at each side, from the front to towards the centre-back, as you steam. Turn the collar and do the same with the stand. Fold the collar round a tailor's ham (see p. 11), stab in a pin at the centre-front to hold it and steam the roll line of the collar to set in the crease. Allow the collar to dry completely before you remove it.

Fusible canvas can also be used for the collar and it should follow the grain line, but it is not pad stitched. Cut away the seam turnings round the collar edge and fuse the canvas to the under collar using a damp cloth, a hot iron and heavy pressure.

To give extra support to the stand of the collar, cut a second piece of fusible canvas to the shape of the stand as far as the roll line and fuse it on top of the first. Cut this second layer without a centre seam by cutting the piece on the bias. The under collar is then shaped as above.

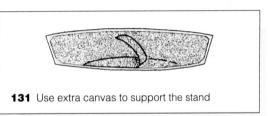

**131** Use extra canvas to support the stand

## ATTACHING THE COLLAR

Attaching the under collar to the coat or jacket is done in the same way as any roll collar with revers. Snip the neck curve of the coat to the stay-stitching line and straighten it out a little. With the right sides together tack the under collar to the neck edge making sure that you align the centre-fronts, shoulders and any large dots exactly.

Stitch the neck seam precisely to the dot marked on the pattern (the outer seam line of the under collar). Clip the jacket seam line almost to the stitching at this point and press the back neck seam open.

Put on the jacket to find the roll line for the lapel, that is, where the lapel folds back to form the rever. Mark this line with chalk.

Cut a length of seam tape to stretch from

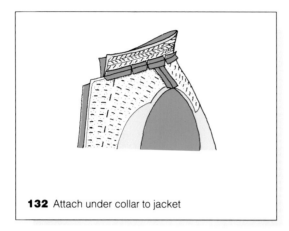

**132** Attach under collar to jacket

the start of the roll of the lapel at the top button to the neck seam. Position the tape 6 mm ($\frac{1}{4}$ in) away from the roll line towards the side seam. Tack the tape in position stretching the tape as you work. This encourages the lapel to roll back on itself. Hem both sides of the tape to the canvas.

At this stage in making up the coat or jacket

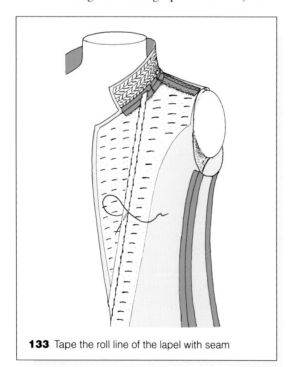

**133** Tape the roll line of the lapel with seam

always keep it on a dressmaker's dummy or a coat hanger with a neck, so that you do not lose the collar shaping.

Holding the lapel into a curve over your forefinger, pad stitch the canvas to the lapel in parallel lines, up and down.

The upper collar and facings are joined next. Stay stitch the neck curves of the front and back facings and clip the seam turnings to the stitching line. This will allow them to straighten out so that they are easier to attach. Join the facings at the shoulder seams and press the seams open.

Pin the upper collar to the facing and check

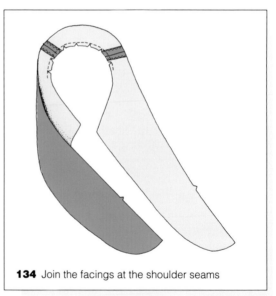

**134** Join the facings at the shoulder seams

the position of the notches with the diagrams on your instruction sheet. It is very easy to accidentally pin the collar upside down at this stage!

Stitch the collar to the facings, finishing the stitching, as before, exactly at the dots marked. Clip the seam turning of the front facing to the stitching line at the dot. Press the seam open.

With the right sides together place the top

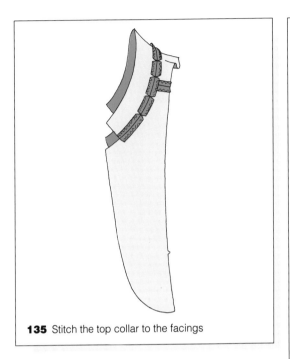

**135** Stitch the top collar to the facings

**136** Stitch the collar and front edges in two stages

collar and facing over the under collar and jacket, matching up seams, notches and thread marks exactly. Tack round the outside edges.

Stitch the lapels in two stages. First, stitch the collar round the outer edges between the two dots. Then, stitch the coat front lapels, beginning the stitching exactly at this same dot and continuing the stitching down the coat front edges.

If you are quite sure of the finished jacket length, the lower edge of the front facing can also be neatened at this stage. Put a tacking line in at the jacket hem line. Stitch across the edge of the facing on this line.

This next stage is vital to the tailored appearance of your jacket. Trim down and layer all the outer seams. Cut off the corners of the collar right to the stitching line. If the lower edge is stitched, cut away the surplus fabric. Turn the collar and facing to the inside. Edge tack right round the jacket,

rolling the seam line between the forefinger and thumb of the other hand, so that it is right on the edge as you tack.

Pin the two collar back neck seams on top of each other and stab stitch invisibly through the seam lines along the back neck between the shoulder seams. Catch stitch the loose edge of the facing to the canvas. (See fig. 137 overleaf)

Pressing is very important at this stage. Use a damp muslin cloth and a steam iron to press the outer edges of the facings very firmly. Press from the right side, then the wrong side, finishing the pressing with a dry cloth. Do not move the jacket until the area you are pressing has dried. Leave the edge tacking in place until the final top-stitching is complete and then, if necessary, press lightly to remove any imprint left over from the tacking.

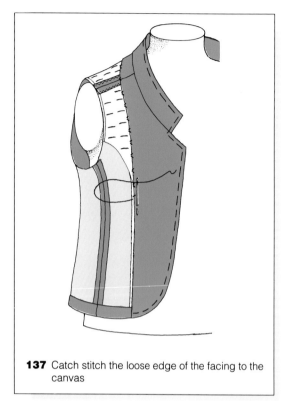

**137** Catch stitch the loose edge of the facing to the canvas

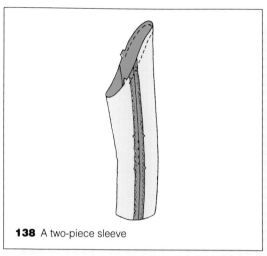

**138** A two-piece sleeve

## A TWO-PIECE SLEEVE

A tailored jacket sleeve is different from the usual sleeve in that it is cut in two pieces which are slightly shaped to the bend of the arm. A small amount of extra fullness is added to the upper sleeve at the elbow and this is eased in to fit the under sleeve.

The two-piece sleeve is inserted into the armhole in the same way as a one piece sleeve, but more care is needed to get the sleeve head smoothly rounded.

Stitch the sleeve seams and press them open using a seam roll (see p. 42). Insert the sleeve as far as the fitting stage and make any necessary adjustments to the armhole line. Check the sleeve line and that the fullness over the sleeve head is evenly dis-

tributed. Also check that the sleeve is hanging correctly. Mark the required sleeve length and take out the sleeve again.

Place the fullness of the seam-turning over the edge of the ironing board or a tailor's ham. Place a damp cloth over the tip of the steam iron and gently steam the fullness in the seam allowance only, so that it becomes slightly damp and will shrink. At this stage nudge the yarns together with the point of the iron so that the fabric is smooth and flat; dry off the wool.

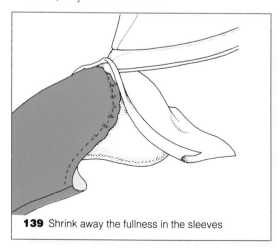

**139** Shrink away the fullness in the sleeves

You cannot do this with synthetic fibres which will not shrink and some wool mixtures may not shrink completely flat. If some fullness is still left in the seam turning and shows as wrinkles on the right side, stitch a strip of wadding on top of the seam turning and under the sleeve head. Do this after re-inserting the sleeve, and make the wadding the same width as the seam turning.

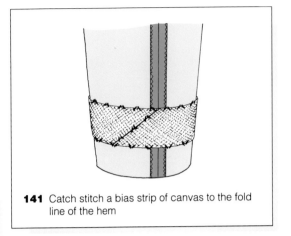

**141** Catch stitch a bias strip of canvas to the fold line of the hem

**140** Stitch a strip of wadding over the seam turning for fabric which cannot be shrunk

Turn up the hem over the canvas and catch stitch the edge of the hem to the canvas. Fusible canvas is attached to the hem turning and not the fabric of the sleeve. Press the edge of the sleeve hem and reinsert the sleeve.

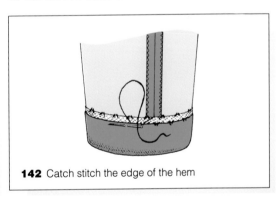

**142** Catch stitch the edge of the hem

The sleeve hem is easier to stitch before the sleeve is reinserted, especially if it has a vent with buttons. The edge of the hem is interfaced to give a crisp edge and the interfacing also takes the hem stitching to avoid a ridge on the right side.

Cut a bias strip of canvas 5 cm (2 in) wide. Lap this round the sleeve with the lower edge to the fold line of the hem. Catch stitch loosely on both edges.

The sleeve cap in some fabrics may need support if it tends to fall inwards at the top, thereby forming dents. Special interfacing with shaped sleeve-heads are now available for this. They follow the contours of the sleeve line and are more satisfactory than a strip of lambswool which dressmakers used before they were developed.

Fit the contours of the sleeve shaper to the sleeve head, allowing it to hang down into

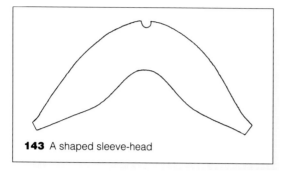

**143** A shaped sleeve-head

the top of the sleeve. Stitch it to the seam turnings.

The jacket hem is also interfaced with a bias strip of canvas placed to the fold line and catch-stitched in the same way as the sleeve hem.

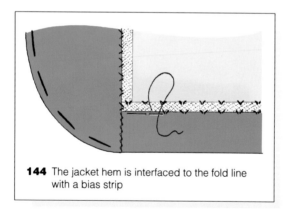

**144** The jacket hem is interfaced to the fold line with a bias strip

Fusible canvas is attached to the inside of the turning of the jacket hem and not to the body of the jacket.

## LINING A JACKET

The facings in a tailored jacket are secured to the interfacing so that the jacket keeps its shape. This means that the lining will have to be stitched by hand. This makes a very neat

and well fitting lining which is also secured at the hem.

A separate pattern is usually given for the lining. It gives a pleat at the centre back and allows for the depth of the pads at the shoulder. However, if no lining is given in your pattern you will find that making a lining pattern for an unlined jacket is quite simple.

To cut the front lining pattern, pin the facing pattern under the front pattern matching outside seam lines, notches etc. Trace down the inner curved edge of the facing. Remove the facing pattern.

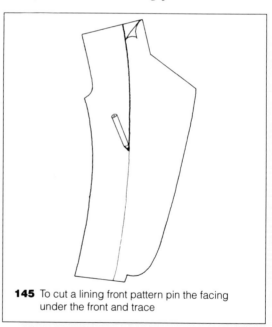

**145** To cut a lining front pattern pin the facing under the front and trace

You now need to add two seam allowances – one seam allowance to turn under to neaten the edge and one seam allowance for the amount the lining will overlap the jacket facing. Draw a line parallel to the first and 3 cm ($1\frac{1}{4}$ in) away from it, that is, nearer the front edge. This is the cutting line for the lining front. Allow extra on the shoulder seams for the pads (the exact amount does not matter as this is fitted accurately later). Add the width of two seam allowances and extend the shoulder.

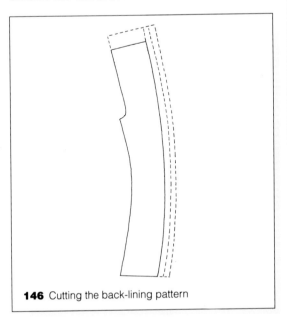

**146** Cutting the back-lining pattern

the inside. Wrap the lining round the jacket, wrong sides together and pin at the armhole edges to hold it.

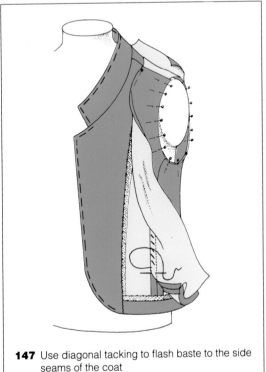

**147** Use diagonal tacking to flash baste to the side seams of the coat

To cut the back-lining pattern, place the back neck facing (if there is one) under the pattern back and draw the shape as above. Add on the turnings. Place the lining pattern 2.5 cm (1 in) away from a fold when cutting out, to allow for the pleat. The sleeve lining is cut from the jacket pattern.

## STITCHING THE LINING

The lining is inserted by hand in two stages – the body and then the sleeves. Join the front and back lining at the side seams. Press the seams open.

Put the jacket wrong side out on a dressmaker's dummy, with the sleeves tucked to

Lift the front lining and fold it towards the back to reveal the side seams. Flash baste the nearest seam turnings of the coat and lining together with diagonal tacking so that the seams are facing and on top of each other.

Then tack the jacket and lining armhole edges together, matching seams and notches. This tacking is not removed, so use a matching thread, a small stitch, and work the row of stitches on the seam allowance just outside the stitching line. Slip stitch the front and back together at the shoulder seam, trimming away the surplus fabric.

Turn under the seam allowance round the

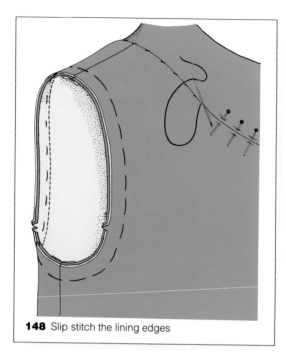

**148** Slip stitch the lining edges

The lining sleeve is stitched last. Stitch the lining sleeve seams and press them open. With both the jacket sleeve and the lining sleeve wrong side out place the front lining seam flat on top of the corresponding jacket sleeve. Match the notches and flash baste the turnings down one edge with diagonal tacking, in the same way as the jacket side seams.

Slip your hand into the lining sleeve, grasp the edge of the jacket sleeve and turn the lining sleeve right side out, over the fabric sleeve.

Turn under the seam allowance round the sleeve head and pin the folded edge over the armhole seam line. Slip stitch in place, taking small tucks over the sleeve head to dispose of surplus fullness.

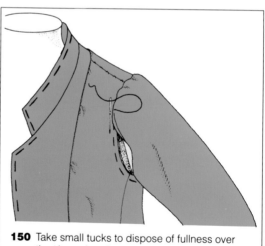

**150** Take small tucks to dispose of fullness over the sleeve head

neck edge and down the front edges and pin. Slip stitch (see p. 41) these lining edges invisibly and firmly to the jacket.

Smooth the lining over the jacket and tack it down just above the hem edge. Turn under the 1.5 cm ($\frac{5}{8}$ in) seam allowance and pin the fold to cover the hem edge so that the excess fabric forms a tuck for wearing ease. Slip stitch the hem.

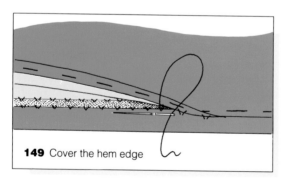

**149** Cover the hem edge

## CHAPTER TEN

# WHAT IS OVERLOCKING?

*Types of overlocker*

*Threading the overlocker*

*Overlocking – basic techniques*

*Overlock stitches*

*Overlocked seams*

verlocking or serging is an excit-ing development for the home dressmaker. It isn't a new tech-nique because overlock machines have always been used in factories for ready-to-wear clothes. What is new, however, is that leading machine manu-facturers now include at least one overlock model in their range for the domestic market and the sales of overlock machines are soaring. It does not, however, replace a conventional machine. It is used in conjunction with it and you must be able to sew before you can fully appreciate its uses.

The overlock machine cannot sew the normal single line of locked machine stitching. It has no bobbin; it has either one or two loopers and knife blades, which cut the fabric cleanly before the needle (or needles) and loopers overcast the edge with a knitting process to finish it. The machine will hold up to four large cones of overlocking thread for this. It also stitches all types of fabric, from sheers to tweeds, and they will feed into the machine evenly without the need to lift the presser foot.

The benefit of an overlocker is that it gives a very professional finish while also being very fast. It also makes possible a great number of short cuts in the construction of a garment and opens up endless possibilities in stretch fabric, and for making leisure wear and children's clothes.

# TYPES OF OVERLOCK MACHINE

## THE 2-THREAD OVERLOCKER

This has one looper and one needle. The 2-thread overlocker is simply an edge overlock machine. The seam is first stitched and then overlocked. It requires two operations.

With this type the looper goes over the top of the fabric and the thread of the looper interlocks with the needle thread. Then the looper goes under the fabric, picks up the needle thread and pulls it to the edge. This can be clearly seen when you use two contrasting threads.

## THE 3-THREAD OVERLOCKER

The 3-thread overlocker has the advantage over the 2-thread machine in that it stitches the seam at the same time as overlocking the edge. It is one operation.

It has one needle and two loopers. The loopers overlock at the seam edge and the needle thread overlocks with both at the seamline.

## THE 3/4-THREAD OVERLOCKER

This is the most versatile of all the overlockers. It has two loopers and two needles. It forms the stitch in the same way as the 3-thread, but there is an extra needle which gives a second line of stitching for extra strength. Both these needle threads interlock with the upper and lower loopers. The term 3/4 means that you can use the machine as a strong 4-thread seam, or, drop one needle and use it as a 3-thread.

## DIFFERENTIAL FEED

Some overlockers have a differential feed. The machine has two feed dogs, one behind the other. For normal sewing these feed through the two layers of fabric at the same rate. Adjusting the differential feed alters the rate at which the fabric is fed through. For example, set on 2, the front feed dog will feed through twice as much fabric under the presser foot as is released by the rear feed dog. This prevents stretching in jersey fabric.

# THREADING THE OVERLOCKER

Threading your overlocker is not difficult; fiddly and time-consuming it may be, but it really isn't difficult.

There should be a colour-coded guide on your machine so follow the manufacturer's instructions exactly. The sequence in which the needles are threaded is vital so refer to the machine manual for the exact threading details.

For the first threading of your machine, it is a good idea to complete it in the same colours that are used on the coloured guide. This simplifies your first threading. If your fingers are not very agile, attach a short length of fine fuse wire to the end of the thread twisting them together to give a secure join. This will help to make the initial threading easier.

After this initial threading you may never need to re-thread your machine again! To change the colour of any of the threads, clip the thread just above the spool. Replace the spool with the new colour, and tie the end of this thread to the loose end of the original thread.

*Have a close look at the overlocked edge!* It will save you a great deal of confusion if you now take a few minutes to identify the threads – which is the upper looper thread and which the lower looper – and then trace them back through the tension discs to the respective loopers. Notice how the needle thread interlocks with these. If you know which thread is which you can avoid threading the wrong needle or looper; this is especially helpful when you come to decorative stitching.

You will notice that only the needle thread penetrates the fabric. The looper threads simply wrap over the edge and are held in place by the needle thread. This is why an overlocker feeds any type of fabric evenly without puckering and does not distort the edge.

An overlocker seam will vary in its make-up depending on which type of machine you have – 2-thread, 3-thread or 4-thread.

Take time to learn the relative position of the threads and colours on your machine as they correspond to the seam stitching. In the seam the upper looper thread provides the most pronounced stitching on the face of the fabric, and is uppermost as you sew; most of the lower looper thread is underneath.

# OVERLOCKING BASICS

## SECURING THE ENDS OF OVERLOCK STITCHING

The easiest way to secure either end of a seam is simply to separate the ends of the chain and tie them in a knot. There is also a fabric adhesive on the market, which is colourless when dry, and is sold for the purpose of sealing the ends of an overlocked seam. In this case the chain can be cut at the end of the seam and a dab of adhesive applied to the thread ends.

## ▶ SECURING THE START OF A SEAM

The best way to secure the end of an overlocked seam is to backstitch it. Make sure there is at least 5 cm (2 in) of chain behind the needle. Take a stitch or two at the start of the seam, just to anchor it. Lift the presser foot, bring the chain out to the left and under the presser foot, place it just to the left of the knife blade (where the overlocking stitches will cover it) and lower the presser foot. Stitch over the chain. After about 2.5 cm (1 in) of stitching draw the chain to the right and the knife will cut off the surplus.

## ▶ SECURING THE END OF A SEAM

Backstitching is also the best and quickest method to use at the end of the seam. Just sew one stitch off the end of the seam, lift the presser foot and ease the stitches off the stitch prong. Flip the work over so that the underside is uppermost and it is now at the front of the machine. Lower the presser foot and stitch about 2.5 cm (1 in), (taking care not to cut the existing stitches), angle the stitching off the seam and move the chain under the knife blade to cut it.

If you forget to go through this procedure at any time, keep a tapestry needle handy. This has a large eye and a blunt end. Thread the chain through the needle and weave the chain back through the overlocking on the fabric.

## UNPICKING OVERLOCK STITCHING

Because overlocked seams are so narrow, you can usually just trim off the seam when you make a mistake. On the few instances where you may not want to do this you can unravel the stitching, which is quite easy to do.

Slip the point of a seam ripper between the overlocking and the fabric and slit along the loops. Then tug the needle thread sharply on each side of the fabric and it will come out fairly easily.

## THE THREAD TO USE

You can, in fact, use any thread on an overlocker – even colour matching is not as important as it is with an ordinary machine. However, special overlocking thread is preferable to ordinary types. This is because overlocking thread is finer than normal thread and has a special finish to make it smoother (so it pulls through all the guides and tension discs on the machine). It is also stronger so it can withstand the heat caused by the speed of sewing and the looping and overlocking actions.

Overlocking uses a vast amount of thread. The spools of overlock thread are therefore larger and, by comparison, they are cheaper than the conventional spool. However, spool adaptors and spool wedges are supplied with overlock sewing machines to enable you to use ordinary sewing thread on them.

Try out the stitching on a scrap of firm fabric before sewing with it on your chosen fabric. Place the fabric to the toe of the presser foot; it is not necessary to lift the foot each time with an overlock machine as it has a very long feed dog. When you come to the end of the fabric, continue to sew, forming a chain at least 10 cm (4 in) long. This is known as chaining off. It is always done each time you finish a length of stitching. Cut the 10 cm (4 in) chain, leaving half attached to the fabric and half on the machine.

# OVERLOCK STITCHES
## THE STITCH LENGTH

Different effects can be achieved by adjusting the stitch length on your overlocker, and these effects can be achieved regardless of which type of thread you use. It is a simple adjustment, usually with a dial or lever, but as a general rule the smaller the number, the closer the stitch (refer to your machine manual). A closed satin stitch is formed by closing up the stitch using an embroidery thread or a buttonhole twist. This makes a very good edge which resembles piping. If you make the stitches further apart by adjusting the stitch length to a higher number, you will get quite a different effect.

Experiment with the stitch length and different combinations of threads – you will be delighted by the variety of effects you can achieve.

## THE STITCH WIDTH

When the stitch width as well as the length is adjusted it gives a narrow hem, with infinite possibilities. The width of the stitch is determined by the stitch-forming prong on the throat plate. To alter the stitch width you can use the alternative throat plate which has a narrower prong. (Consult your machine manual for instructions on changing the throat plate.)

## A NARROW ROLLED HEM

If you tighten the upper looper thread on a narrow hem, the tighter thread will cause the edge to curl. This, combined with the closed-up stitch length, will give a narrow, rolled hem with a satin stitch edge. A picot edge is achieved if you do not close up the stitch length.

The fabric rolls to the underside of the fabric and at the same time the upper looper thread is pulled right round the edge of the fabric, again to the underside of the fabric. The needle and lower looper thread should merge together in a perfect rolled hem.

### ▶ SCARVES AND SHAWLS

These need a very durable hem which will stand up to the unavoidable demands of being

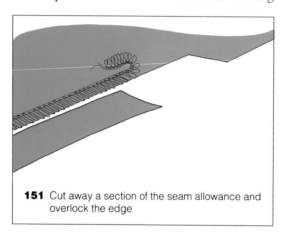

**151** Cut away a section of the seam allowance and overlock the edge

pulled and knotted. For scarves and shawls, choose a fabric which has very little difference in the right and wrong sides and preferably a wool challis, fine cotton or silk.

**Cutting Out**

You can gently round off the corners of the scarves to make stitching easier.

- Scarf – cut a 70 cm (27 in) square
- Shawl – cut a 102 cm (40 in) square

Cut away a 2.5 cm (1 in) section of the seam allowance. Lift the presser foot and line up the edge of the cut edge with the knife blade. Overlock the edge and once you are back to

where you started, raise the knife blade and overlap two or three stitches.

The join in the overlock stitching on the scarf must be perfect. To achieve a very neat finish on a narrow hem lift the presser foot, leaving the needle in the work. Flip the fabric back on itself and to the left. Lower the presser foot and stitch-off the edge. A dab of seam sealant will secure the thread ends. Alternatively, separate the threads and weave them individually into the hem.

### ▶ BRAIDING

With an overlocker you can even make braid. Use a 6 mm ($\frac{1}{4}$ in) wide ribbon in the colour required. Thread the loopers with lustrous embroidery thread and stitch over the ribbon without cutting it, allowing the needle to drop off at each side of the ribbon.

# OVERLOCKED SEAMS

In general, the overlocked seam is used for clothes which are loosely fitting and the seams do not need to be pressed open, e.g. for children's clothes, lingerie and knits. The flat seam, with the edges overlocked, is used for bulky fabric, e.g. tweeds and all closely fitting styles where the overlocked seam would form a ridge. Any fabric which gives you problems with the stitching on your regular machine will be handled beautifully on an overlocker. You may need to use both types of seam in the same garment, e.g. overlocked seams on a full skirt with a flat seam where the zip is inserted.

## OVERLOCKED SEAMS

Even where no fitting is required on a skirt, it is still important to take the correct seam allowance. The stitching line is where the needle penetrates the fabric and *not* where the knife cuts.

## FLAT SEAMS

It saves time to overlock all seam edges before the garment is put together. Obviously it is a waste of time to overlock some edges – such as waist edges which will be covered by a band – and hem edges if these are to be straightened and re-cut.

Two or three threads at the most should be used to overlock the seam edges. Drop one thread on a four-thread overlocker.

## FLATLOCKED SEAMS

Flatlocking is the term used when two edges are overlocked using a fairly loose stitch tension. The seam is then opened out and the two layers of fabric pulled apart to flatten the seam. The resulting flat seam is decorative on both sides with loops on one side and a ladder stitch on the other. Either side can be

used as the right side, depending on the effect you prefer.

The best flatlocking effect is achieved on a two-thread overlocker. The tensions on a three-thread overlocker must be loosened as much as possible so that the loops and the ladder stitches are the same width. A four-thread overlocker is not suitable for flatlocking as the seam edges will not pull apart sufficiently.

Press under the seam turnings on both of the edges which are to be joined. Place the fabric pieces with the wrong sides together (this gives the loops on the right side when finished). Lift the knife blade, or use a flatlock plate guide depending on your machine, and overlock the edges of the fabric.

Ease the two layers of fabric apart until the seam lies flat. To make a very decorative seam, thread the looper(s) with embroidery thread, top-stitching thread, *cotton à broder* (embroidery cotton) or very narrow ribbon. Use regular overlocking thread or buttonhole twist in the needle.

Flatlocking can also be worked simply as a decorative row of stitching on the surface of the fabric and not necessarily joining a seam. This is known as decorative flatlock.

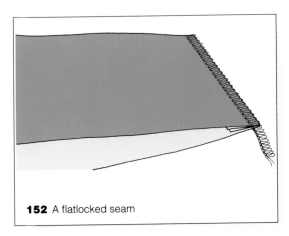

**152** A flatlocked seam

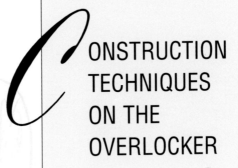

## CHAPTER ELEVEN

# CONSTRUCTION TECHNIQUES ON THE OVERLOCKER

*Making a skirt*

*Making a skirt lining*

*Decorative hemming on an overlocker*

*Making a blouse*

*Making an unlined jacket*

An overlock machine gives another dimension to dressmaking. It will eliminate much of the hand sewing you do using an ordinary sewing machine – and it's even more fun! The time you take to make a skirt can be cut by half, using an overlocker.

You will first have to decide which type of seam you will use: an overlocked seam, with both edges overlocked and trimmed together at 6 mm ($\frac{1}{4}$ in), or conventional flat seam with the 1.5 cm ($\frac{5}{8}$ in) turnings pressed open and only the seam edges overlocked.

It will all depend on your choice of fabric. For a T-shirt in single jersey, for example, you would use the quickest method of stitching – the narrow overlocked seam. For an unlined jacket in a wool double jersey you would use the conventional flat seam, pressed open.

Both types of seam may be used in the same garment. A cotton skirt can be made with overlocked seams but with a flat zip seam with 1.5 cm ($\frac{5}{8}$ in) turnings.

An overlocker will certainly make your dressmaking quicker and this chapter shows you some of the short cuts which are possible with overlocking.

# MAKING A SKIRT

## POCKETS

If your skirt has a pocket in a side seam, you will come across a difficulty with overlocking the seams. The lower edge of the standard shape of pocket, which is attached to the side seam, has a concave corner. Since the knife of the overlock machine cuts before the edge is overlocked, take care not to cut too far into the seam.

On a casual cotton skirt or on children's clothes a quick patch pocket can be made by overlocking round the pocket edges and then top stitching the piece to the skirt with regular machine stitching. (See the section on the unlined jacket, p. 121.)

## THE WAISTBAND

A waistband can be overlocked to the skirt and this avoids any hand sewing inside the band.

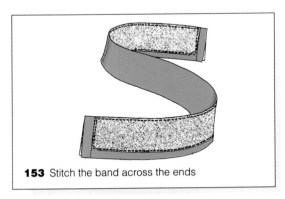

**153** Stitch the band across the ends

Interface the band in the usual way, then fold it in half along its length and stitch across the two short ends. Next trim the seams and turn the band to the right side. Press the ends and the fold line. Try on the band to make sure that it is the correct size for your waist, at the same time allowing for an overlap.

Pin both open edges of the band to the waist of the skirt. Overlock the edge, including the overlap, before securing the chain. Press the seam downwards, away from the waistband edge and towards the skirt and then hand hem the narrow overlocked turning to the zip tape.

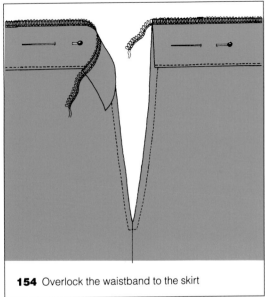

**154** Overlock the waistband to the skirt

## A FIVE-MINUTE SKIRT LINING

Most skirts are improved by a lining and you can make up a straight or A-line skirt lining with a side seam slit in five minutes on your overlocker. You will not need to secure the ends of the chain at all.

To calculate the amount of fabric needed to make the lining, measure the skirt's finished length. You will require this length of a lining fabric in 150 cm (60 in) width. To cut the lining, use a pattern for a straight or an A-line skirt.

## ▶CUTTING OUT

Re-fold the lining fabric with both selvedges to the centrefold-line. Place each back and front skirt pattern-piece to a fold in order to do away with a front and back seam. Cut out the lining. Stitch the waist darts using your ordinary machine. Alternatively, form the waist-shaping with small unpressed pleats. Next, place the front and back pieces so that the right sides are together and then overlock the right hand seam.

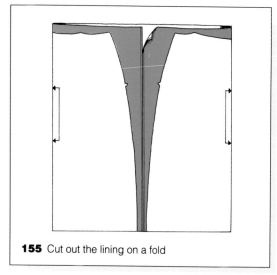

**155** Cut out the lining on a fold

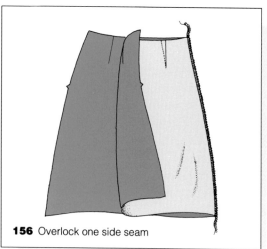

**156** Overlock one side seam

Now overlock only down the length of the zip opening and on the single layer of the left side seam, tapering off the edge.

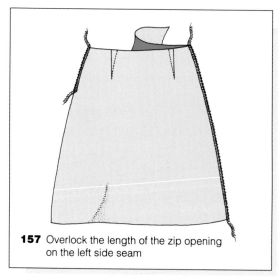

**157** Overlock the length of the zip opening on the left side seam

Starting at the waist, overlock down the length of the zip on the opposite seam edge. Lift the presser foot, place both seam edges together, lower the presser foot and continue to overlock in order to join the side seam.

**158** Stop overlocking 20 cm (8 in) from the hem

116

Stop about 20 cm (8 in) from the hem. Lift the presser foot and fold one layer of fabric out of the way.

Continue overlocking the single fabric. Stitch around the corner at the hemline in a curve. Continue stitching right round the hem edge, curving the second corner at the

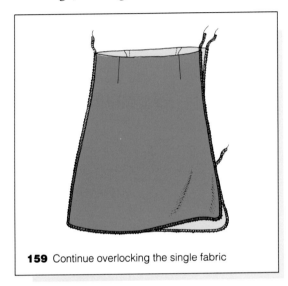

**159** Continue overlocking the single fabric

hem, to return to the side seam. Stitch up the side seam to the point where the seams join and stitch over the join to secure the threads.

Tack together the waist edges of the lining and the skirt after inserting the skirt zip but before attaching the band. Overlock the lining, skirt, and band, together – as in fig. 154.

# THE HEM

Overlocked hems are very neat and they considerably speed up the process of finishing the skirt. Even if you do the final stitching by hand, the overlocker cuts off the surplus fabric and neatens the edge in one operation.

However, you will still have to mark the finished length carefully and choose the correct hem finish for the type of skirt fabric you are using. In casual clothes and some knit fabrics, you may find that you can leave an overlocked edge as the finished hem, without any further turning.

In most fabric, however, the hem is done in two stages: the fold line of the finished hem is measured, and then the surplus fabric is cut off to give an even seam allowance.

The fold line of the hem is best marked with thread or pressed in lightly with the iron. The cutting line of the hem must also be marked to keep it straight as you overlock. The depth of the turning you allow will vary according to the fabric and whether it is to be finished by hand or machine. Measure the required hem allowance down from the fold line and mark it at intervals with chalk.

## ▶ HEMS ON STRAIGHT SKIRTS
Allow a 4 cm ($1\frac{1}{2}$ in) hem turning. Overlock the edge then turn up the hem and catch stitch invisibly, by hand (see p. 41).

## ▶ HEMS ON FULL SKIRTS
Allow only a 1 cm ($\frac{3}{8}$ in) hem turning. Overlock the edge, right side uppermost. Turn up the hem and stitch on the regular machine, 6 mm ($\frac{1}{4}$ in) from the fold.

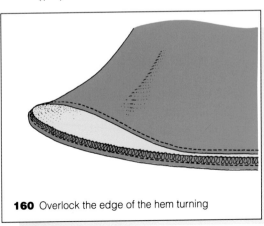

**160** Overlock the edge of the hem turning

*117*

### ▶ HEMS ON LONG SKIRTS AND BRIDAL WEAR

Allow a 1 cm ($\frac{3}{8}$ in) hem stitching. Overlock the edge. Turn the hem to the inside and stitch using your ordinary machine with a good match of thread, right on the fold of the hem as close to the edge as possible.

# MAKING A BLOUSE

An overlocker reduces the time to make a blouse and it gives you scope to adapt your pattern with a wide choice of decorative finishes.

## TUCKS

Pin tucks or wider decorative tucks look good worked parallel to the centre-front of a blouse. The best way is to tuck the fabric for each front separately. Do this before you cut out the fronts. Next, place the blouse front on the fabric and mark the centre line and the fold line of the front edge with thread.

Bearing in mind that the centre-front lines lie on top of each other when the blouse is fastened, plan the position and number of tucks required. Draw them lightly with chalk and a ruler. Fold the fabric right side to the outside along the line of the tuck and press each one.

Thread the loopers of the overlocker with shiny embroidery thread, buttonhole twist, or regular matching or contrast thread. Experiment on a scrap of fabric using both the regular stitch width and the narrow-hemming plate. Delicate fabric looks best tucked with the narrow hem and sturdier fabric can take very bold tucks. *Lift the knife blade* and overlock down the fold of the tuck. Press the tucks, then place the pattern piece on the tucked fabric and cut out.

## THE COLLAR

The collar gives you another opportunity for trying out the various decorative edges on the overlocker.

Sandwich the interfacing between the upper and under collar with the right side

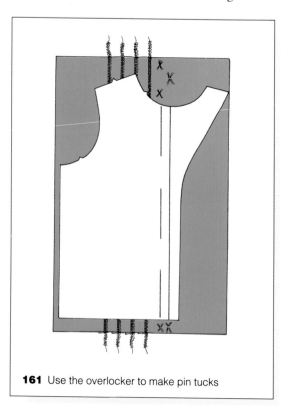

**161** Use the overlocker to make pin tucks

out. Overlock the collar edge, using the narrow hem and decorative thread (see p. 109). Close up the stitch length to give a close satin stitch. Gently round off the corners. Alternatively, stitch the collar in the usual way, using the regular machine.

Attaching a collar using an overlocker is quick and easy. It eliminates the need for a back neck facing and for any hand sewing at all.

First overlock the outer edges of the front

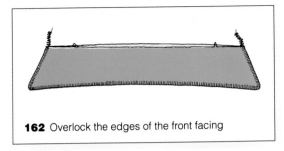

**162** Overlock the edges of the front facing

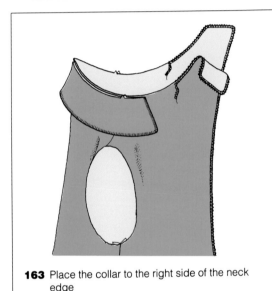

**163** Place the collar to the right side of the neck edge

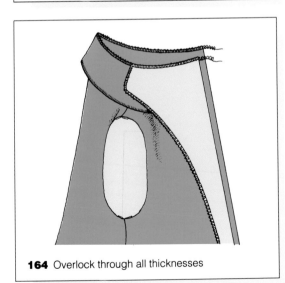

**164** Overlock through all thicknesses

facing. Place the collar to the right side of the neck edge, matching notches and shoulder marks. Fold the front facing along the fold line over the edges of the collar and tack. Overlock through all thicknesses. Turn the facings to the inside and press.

# THE CUFF OPENING

Hand sewing can also be eliminated on the cuff and cuff opening. On children's blouses it is quite acceptable to cut the slit for the cuff opening, straighten it out and just over-lock the edge. For a better finish, cut the opening and a strip of fabric the length of the opening and 3 cm ($1\frac{1}{4}$ in) wide.

Press the strip in half lengthwise and place it on the right side of the fabric at the edge of the opening. Overlock the edge with the slit uppermost, skimming the fabric rather than cutting it and easing out the fold at the base of the slit.

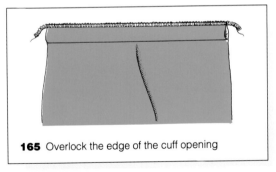

**165** Overlock the edge of the cuff opening

Fold the strip to the inside and press the band under, on the overlap of the cuff. Stitch across the fold of the strip at the base on the regular machine.

▶ATTACHING THE CUFF
Hand sewing can also be eliminated on the cuff by using your overlock machine.

*119*

Make the cuff in the usual way on the regular machine, or alternatively, the outer edges of the cuff can be finished with a narrow satin stitch, hemming in the same way as the collar.

Gather or pleat the edge of the sleeve according to the pattern. Place the finished cuff, with the open edge to the edge of the sleeve, right sides together. Overlock through all thicknesses and turn the cuff downwards.

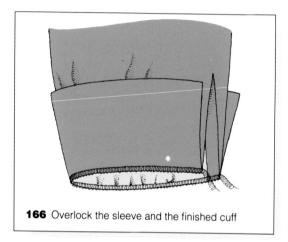

**166** Overlock the sleeve and the finished cuff

### ▶A COMBINED CUFF AND SLIT OPENING

A neat and easy way to attach the cuff is to combine it with a faced slit opening.

Mark the position of the cuff opening on the sleeve. Cut a facing 2.5 cm (1 in) longer than the slit and 5 cm (2 in) wide. Overlock the edges.

Centre the facing over the slit on the right side of the sleeve. Stitch each side of the marked line, tapering to a fine point using the regular machine. Cut between the lines of stitching, but do not turn the facing.

Place the open edge of the completed cuff to the edge of the sleeve, tucking it under the slit facing at each end. Overlock the edge through all thicknesses.

Turn the cuff downwards and the slit facing to the inside of the sleeve and press.

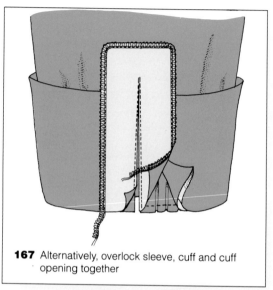

**167** Alternatively, overlock sleeve, cuff and cuff opening together

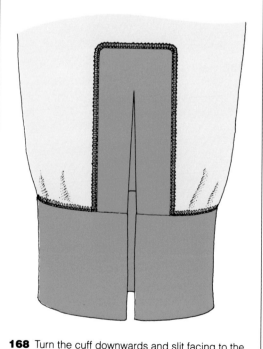

**168** Turn the cuff downwards and slit facing to the inside of the sleeve

# MAKING AN UNLINED JACKET

An overlocker is a boon for making up an unlined jacket. The overlocked edges make the jacket look very professional.

As with the blouse, you can change the order in which you join the pieces to give a much speedier construction. Whereas with a blouse you will generally use the narrow overlocked seam, with a jacket it will probably be the stitched seam, pressed open with the edges overlocked, that you will use.

Overlock all the edges that require it at the outset and while the fabric is flat. This means overlocking any seams which are to be pressed open, e.g. the side seams, the underarm seams of the sleeve, and the shoulder seams. Also, overlock the inner edges of the front facings and the top of the pocket and the hem of the sleeve. Remember to just

skim the edge of the seam, so that you do not trim off the seam allowance. Leave the jacket hem, as it is quicker to overlock it all in one after the side seams have been joined. Also, leave the armhole edges as these will be overlocked together with the sleeve armhole edges.

Tack the interfacing to the facings and overlock the two edges together. If interfacing is to be added inside the sleeve hem, add this in with the overlocked edge also and on the wrong side of the fabric.

The jacket shoulder seams can then be stitched on your ordinary machine and pressed open. Make up and top-stitch the collar in the usual way. In a pattern where the front facings are cut in one with the jacket, the collar can be attached in the same way as the blouse collar, thereby eliminating the hand sewing (see p. 118).

▶ SINGLE LAYER CONSTRUCTION

This method, eliminating facings, is also possible with a decorative technique and using a firm fabric such as double-face wool, flannel or firmly woven linen types.

1 Overlock the collar and pocket edges, rounding off the corners and cutting off the

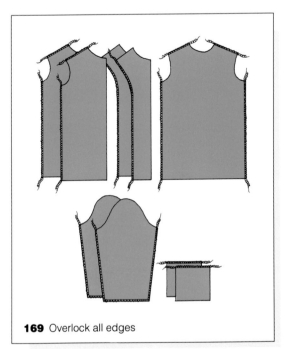

**169** Overlock all edges

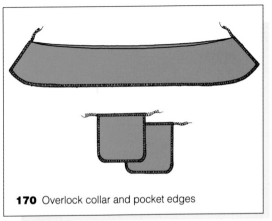

**170** Overlock collar and pocket edges

*121*

correct seam allowance. A double layer of fabric can be used to stiffen the collar if necessary and depending on the fabric used. Stitch the pockets in place on the coat front, using the ordinary machine.

**2** Overlock the shoulder seams. You may even like to put the wrong sides together so that the seams show on the right side.

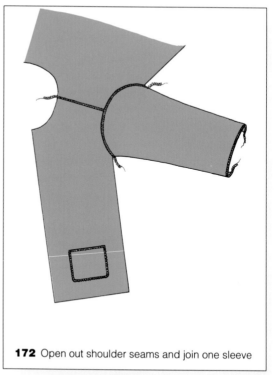

**172** Open out shoulder seams and join one sleeve

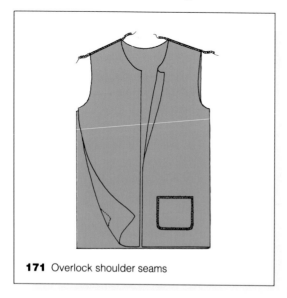

**171** Overlock shoulder seams

**3** Overlock the sleeve hems. Open out the shoulder seams and join one sleeve, the left hand sleeve, to the front and back at the shoulder and overlock the armhole seam.

**4** Join this sleeve and underarm seam, with the fabric right sides together so that this seam is to the inside.

**5** Pin the collar in place at the neck edge. Start at the lower edge of the open side seam and overlock the jacket hem, curving the corner to stitch up one front then along the back neck seam joining in the collar, then down the other front and finally along the jacket hem at the back.

**173** Overlock collar to neck edge and overlock jacket hem

**6** Attach the other sleeve to the shoulder. Join the other side and underarm seam with the right sides together as before.

A coat with a raglan armhole will need both sleeves inserted at stage 3 to complete the curve of the neck. Close the right hand underarm and side seam only, before edging the coat, for ease of construction, and to keep the top looper stitches on the outside of the coat.

Buttonholes on single layer construction will tend to stretch, so the coat is best finished with a zip or as a wrap with a tie belt.

► **TO COVER SHOULDER PADS**
Shoulder pads for an unlined jacket should be covered with the same fabric as that in which the garment has been made. Cut an oval of fabric large enough to wrap around the pad. Lap it over the thick end of the pad then overlock and trim it to size in one operation.

## CHAPTER TWELVE

# SEWING STRETCH FABRIC ON THE OVERLOCKER

▷ *Pressing*

▷ *Knit patterns*

▷ *Cutting out*

▷ *Making perfect seams*

▷ *Ribbing*

▷ *Interfacing*

▷ *Making a sleeveless top*

▷ *Making a skirt*

▷ *Making trousers*

▷ *Making a cardigan jacket*

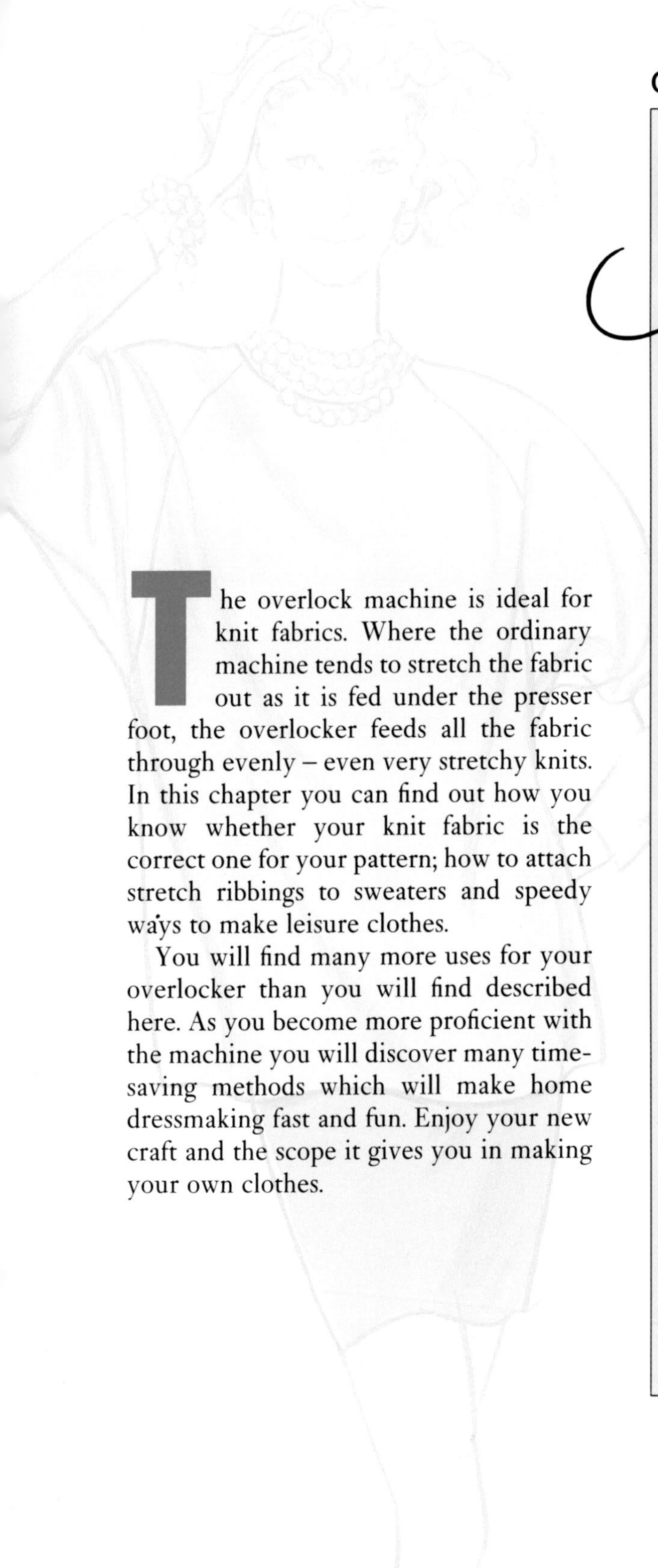

The overlock machine is ideal for knit fabrics. Where the ordinary machine tends to stretch the fabric out as it is fed under the presser foot, the overlocker feeds all the fabric through evenly – even very stretchy knits. In this chapter you can find out how you know whether your knit fabric is the correct one for your pattern; how to attach stretch ribbings to sweaters and speedy ways to make leisure clothes.

You will find many more uses for your overlocker than you will find described here. As you become more proficient with the machine you will discover many time-saving methods which will make home dressmaking fast and fun. Enjoy your new craft and the scope it gives you in making your own clothes.

# PRESSING

Pressing for knit fabric is little and light. Use a steam iron and press the overlocked seam very lightly to one side, holding the iron just above and resting it only very lightly on the stitching. It is rarely necessary to press the seam on the right side and again, hold the iron just above the seam and let the steam do the work. Plain single jerseys, will easily take the imprint of the seam line so press sparingly.

# KNIT PATTERNS

The stretch levels of knit fabrics are roughly categorised as limited stretch; moderate stretch; very stretchy.

There is a gauge on the side of the pattern envelope to test the stretchiness of the fabric. This indicates how far each type of stretch fabric will be expected to 'give', so you can judge the suitability of the fabric you have chosen for that particular pattern.

Take 10 cm (4 in) of fabric. Hold the left hand edge to the left side of the gauge and ease it across the width with your right hand. Stretch the fabric to its limit, without allowing it to curl, to assess the category of the knit. This will indicate the recovery properties of the knit. If it does not recover well, it will probably go baggy with wear.

When your pattern gives a gauge on the side of the envelope it is important to test the fabric you intend to buy against the pattern and make sure that it has the right degree of stretch.

Patterns designed for stretch knits only, have less ease and very little shaping. There are no darts, for example. They use the inherent stretch properties of the fabric for shape and style.

# CUTTING OUT

Always use a 'with nap' layout for cutting knits. Cut out with all the fabric flat on the table. Fabric hanging off the table edge will stretch. If your table is not big enough to accommodate the pattern then fan fold the surplus at one edge. For a simple top like this, facings are omitted and the edge is finished with overlocking.

Use regular overlocking thread in contrast, neutral or matching colours, in the needle(s). Thread the upper looper with decorative thread (rainbow thread is particularly effective) or buttonhole twist, and the lower looper, with regular thread or the same decorative thread. As the inside of the overlocked edge tends to show at the armholes, the same decorative thread looks best.

# MAKING PERFECT SEAMS

Overlockers feed the fabric through evenly and you can achieve perfect seaming on knit fabric.

Pin the fabric right sides together, with the pins parallel to the edge and not, as with regular dressmaking, at right angles to the edge. Keep them well inside the seam line and away from the cutting blades. Until you are confident that you can sew straight lines on your overlocker, draw the seam line on your fabric in soft pencil or chalk and follow the line with the mark on the toe of the presser foot.

Seams in stretch knits are generally overlocked. In heavier stable knits such as wool and double jersey it is better to stitch the seams on an ordinary machine and press them open, overlocking the edges before or after stitching the seam.

## ▶ LETTUCE EDGING

This is a very pretty effect which is suitable for hems on stretch fabrics or soft bias wovens which do not fray readily. The knit fabric is stretched out as you sew, giving a permanently ruffled edge. It works best on lightweight jersey and knits with two-way stretch, which pulls out to give a deeply frilled edge.

It is worked with 2- or 3-thread stitching, using the narrow or rolled hem on the overlocker. Set the stitch to a close satin stitch. Regular thread may be used, but a toning lustrous embroidery thread, or a contrasting overlocking thread gives definition to the edge. Increase the setting of the pressure of the machine foot to encourage the fabric to stretch.

Mark the hem line with chalk. Overlock the edge, with the fabric right side uppermost (with the exception of tricot, which rolls naturally to the wrong side when cut and is placed right side down) and the knife to the chalk line. Gently stretch out the knit fabric *in front* as you feed it in, taking care not to bend the needle.

# RIBBING

This can be purchased by the yard or ready-made into cuffs and bands for finishing sweater hems or necklines.

## A V-SHAPED NECKLINE USING RIBBING

In a stretch knit fabric, a v-neck will stretch as soon as it is picked up after cutting out. It is a good idea to stick transparent tape along the neck edge but away from the stitching line inside the dress or top before you even

lift it from the cutting table. This is more effective than stay stitching.

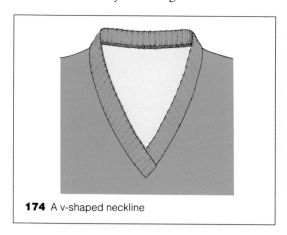

**174** A v-shaped neckline

Measure round the neck and cut a strip of fabric to this length, plus ample turnings to allow for the overlap. Make the width twice the required finished width of the band plus turnings.

Fold the band in half along the length, right side outside, and press lightly. In a very stretchy fabric add a little extra lightweight interfacing inside the band (see p. 129) or tape the neckline as you overlock it.

The seam at the point of the V can be very bulky in a knit fabric and so it is easier to stitch the ends of the band separately.

Make a mark on the left neck edge, the width of the band from the point of the V. Place the band to the neck edge and overlock from this mark around the neck edge. Leave the edge unstitched from the point of the V to the mark.

With the right side uppermost, lap the end of the band on the right side over the band on the other side. Insert the end of this band into the opening. Adjust from the right side so that the bands lie flat. Pin in place.

**175** Overlock fabric to neck edge

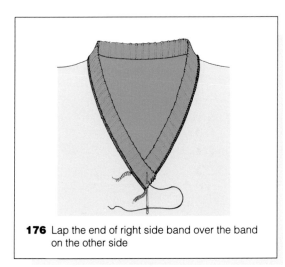

**176** Lap the end of right side band over the band on the other side

Mark the sleeve hem edge and the ribbed cuff into quarters with chalk. Stretch out the cuff and pin it to the right side of the sleeve, matching the marks.

Overlock, keeping the cuff stretched as you sew. Join the underarm sleeve seam after attaching the ribbing.

Ready-made ribbing cuffs will have to be attached after the underarm seam is stitched, stretching out the ribbing as you sew.

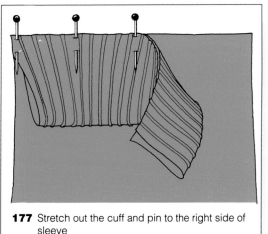

**177** Stretch out the cuff and pin to the right side of sleeve

# INTERFACING

Where to interface and what type of interfacing to use depends on the type and texture of the knit fabric. Stable knits (such as double jersey) will need no interfacing, but the shoulder seams and raglan armhole seams should be taped.

Stretch knits need a very light interfacing. The best type is a very lightweight *stretch* interfacing. This is made specifically for all types of knits to give support to areas which, after repeated stretching, will not return naturally to shape.

Turn the garment to the wrong side. Cut away the surplus fabric on the bands, allowing turnings, overlock the remaining edge of the V and oversew the open edge by hand.

## RIBBING CUFF

Ribbing cuffs are simpler to attach if they are added before the underarm sleeve seam is stitched.

Light, supersoft interfacing is the next best alternative to stretch interfacing.

# MAKING A SLEEVELESS TOP

One of the easiest garments to make with your overlocker is a sleeveless top (single layer fabric) with overlocked edges and no facings.

One of the most exciting things about overlocking is the speed with which you can see the garment taking shape. This type of sleeveless top can be made up in less than an hour.

### ▶ QUICK CONSTRUCTION SEQUENCE

**1** Join one shoulder seam with the right sides together. It is not necessary to secure the ends of the chain at this stage.

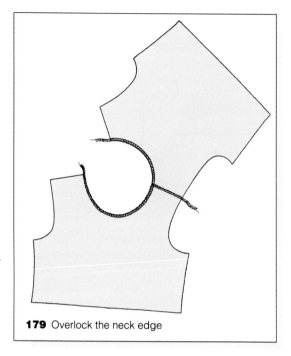

**179** Overlock the neck edge

**3** Join the other shoulder seam.

**4** Overlock the armholes.

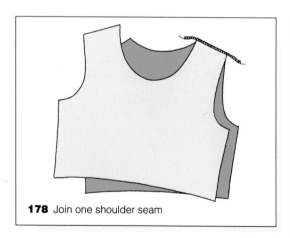

**178** Join one shoulder seam

**2** Overlock the neck edge.

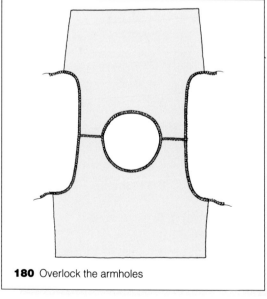

**180** Overlock the armholes

130

**5** Join *one* side seam, securing the chain at the armhole edge.

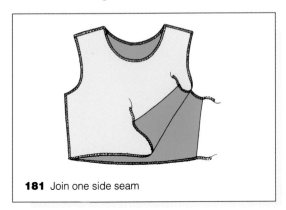

**181** Join one side seam

**6** Overlock the hem.

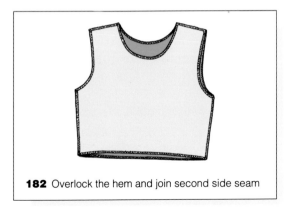

**182** Overlock the hem and join second side seam

**7** Finally join the second side seam, securing the chain at both ends (see p. 108).

# MAKING A SKIRT

A pull-on skirt with an elasticized waist can be made on an overlocker in less than an hour.

There are many skirt patterns for pull-on skirts in knit fabrics. Some have separate waistbands through which the elastic is threaded, while others have the top of the skirt extended and this is folded down to form the casing. This is a simple style which works well.

But the quickest way to make a skirt is to use elasticized facing. This is attached to the top of the skirt and in stretch fabric the wide elastic can be turned up or down to give you the advantage of a variable skirt length. The overlocked seam gives a flat neat finish with the elastic on the inside and can be worn with or without a belt.

▶ CONSTRUCTION SEQUENCE

**1** Join one side seam only and any panel seams.

**2** Cut the elastic facing to fit the waist snugly plus an allowance for turnings. Fold the elastic in half and mark the halfway fold, and fold again and mark the quarters. Mark the top of the skirt in the same way.

**3** Pin or fix the elastic with a quick tack to the inside of the top of the skirt, matching the marks.

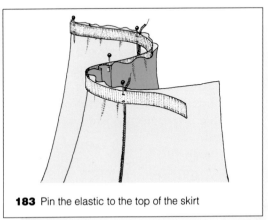

**183** Pin the elastic to the top of the skirt

**4** Stretching out the elastic, overlock the top edge, removing the pins *before you come to them*.

*131*

Keep the edge of the elastic to the left of the cutting blade.

**184** Overlock the side seams

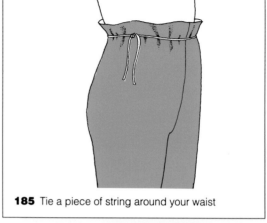

**185** Tie a piece of string around your waist

5 Turn the elastic *upwards* and overlock the other side seam of the skirt.
6 Finish the hem as desired.

A separate waistband on a pull-on skirt is attached in the same way as the band for pull-on trousers.

# MAKING TROUSERS

Pull-on trousers in stretch fabric are very comfortable for leisure wear and the problem of fitting is minimised by using the stretch properties of the fabric. At the cutting out stage allow an extra 5 cm (2 in) or so at the waist edge. Make up the pants as far as the waistband.

## ▶ CONSTRUCTION SEQUENCE

1 Put on the trousers and pull them up until they fit as you want them – sitting as well as standing! Then tie a piece of string around your waist and get help to mark this line with chalk on to the fabric. This will be the cutting line for the overlocker.

2 Next remove the trousers and cut away the excess fabric, leaving a turning of about 1 cm ($\frac{3}{8}$ in). Cut a length of wide elastic to the length of your waist measurement, plus an allowance for turnings. Cut the waistband fabric strip according to the pattern, and make the width 2 cm ($\frac{3}{4}$ in) wider than the elastic.

3 Stitch the short sides of the waistband,

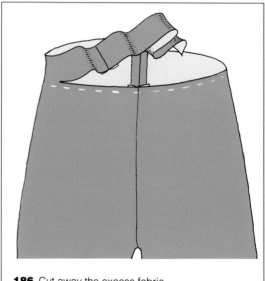

**186** Cut away the excess fabric

right sides together, to form a circle, using your ordinary machine. Fold the band in half along the length and press the fold. Stitch the elastic in a circle and place the edge of the elastic to the fold inside the band. Pin, matching half way and quarters, as below, or tack with diagonal tacking.

4 Place the raw edges of the band to the waist edge of the pants, matching half way

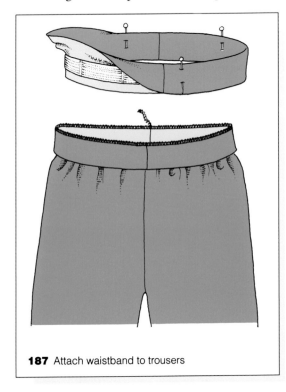

**187** Attach waistband to trousers

and quarters. Overlock through all thicknesses, easing out the elastic and cutting off surplus turnings of 1 cm ($\frac{3}{8}$ in).

# MAKING A CARDIGAN JACKET

An unlined jacket in a knit fabric is a satisfying project on an overlocker. The inside hems

and seams look very neat and the band facings take very little time compared to the usual lengthy procedure on your ordinary machine and finished by hand hemming.

▶ THE CARDIGAN BANDS

The style of a cardigan means that it is very likely to stretch in length in a knit fabric. Depending on the fabric, the bands may also become 'stringy' as they stretch. If the bands are lightly interfaced, they will keep their shape and also support the shape of the front cardigan and neck edges.

Iron-on or sew-in interfacing may be used and the band interfaced to the fold line only, *not* used double. If sew-in interfacing is used, invisibly catch stitch the edge of the interfacing to the fold line.

▶ CONSTRUCTION SEQUENCE

1 Tape and join the shoulder seams.
2 Overlock the edge of the sleeve, turn up the hem and stitch it on the regular machine.
3 Join the sleeves to the body and overlock the armhole.
4 Fold the jacket with the right side inside and place sleeve and side seams together. Overlock the full length of the side seams,

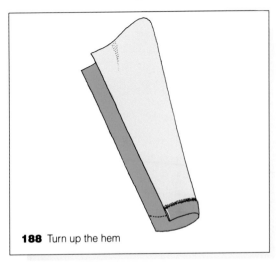

**188** Turn up the hem

continuing down the underarm seam, making sure that the edges of the seam are exactly

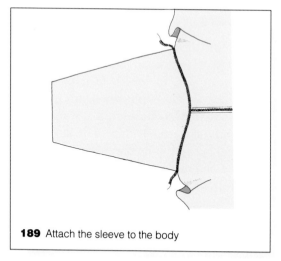

**189** Attach the sleeve to the body

together at the cuff. (It is easier to achieve this by starting at the jacket hem and finishing at the cuff, as the bulk of the sleeve hem can be a problem when starting to sew.)

5  Turn up the jacket hem and stitch this on your ordinary machine.

6  Interface the bands if this is necessary (see above). Join the bands at the centre-back

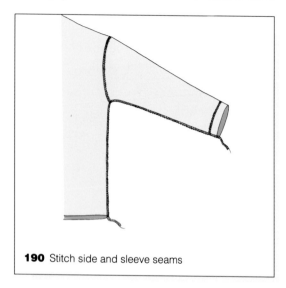

**190** Stitch side and sleeve seams

seam. Fold the ends of the band in half with the right sides together and stitch across the end. Turn the ends right side out and press the fold line along the length of the band.

Place the open edges of the band to the jacket edge, matching the notches. Overlock the raw edges through all thicknesses.

**191** Place the band to the jacket edge

## THE POCKETS

The quickest way to finish the pockets is to leave them flat and overlock the edges. For a multi-coloured wool try using overlocking thread or buttonhole twist in the dominant colour of the jacket. Closing up the stitch length when you do this will create an attractive solid edge.

For an overlocked edge, interface only the top of the pocket and keep the interfacing away from the pocket edge. Apply the interfacing to the wrong side of the upper edge of the top of the pocket. Overlock round the pocket edges. Stitch the pocket flat on to the cardigan fronts sewing around the outer edge using your ordinary machine.

# DRESSMAKER'S DICTIONARY

## A

**Appliqué** – To apply one fabric on top of another, usually with embroidery stitches by hand or machine.

**Asymmetrical** – Lack of symmetry or balance – lop-sided.

## B

**Backing** – A lining fabric used to stabilise another and made up as one with the top fabric.

**Balance lines** – The horizontal line at right angles to the lengthwise grain lines.

**Baste** – to tack

**Bateau** – A boat-shaped neckline.

**Bias** – The true diagonal direction across a fabric at 45 degrees to the selvedge.

**Bias binding** – Strips of fabric cut on the bias for binding edges and curves.

**Blind hemming** – Invisible hem stitching.

**Blouson** – Fullness gathered at the waist or hip and allowed to blouse over or fall loosely.

**Bolero** – Short, above-the-waist jacket – Spanish style.

## C

**Camisole** – Sleeveless top, usually with thin straps.

**Cap sleeve** – Very short cropped set-in sleeve.

**Casing** – A hem through which ribbon or elastic can be threaded.

**Centre-front** – The line on the pattern denoting the exact centre of the bodice. It is important to mark this line on the fabric as it denotes where the right and left fronts overlap.

**Chevron** – Stripes stitched together to form a V-shape.

**Clip** – To cut fabric to allow for easing out on curves and corners.

**Couture** – Design and making of fashionable garments.

**Cowl** – A loosely draped collar.

**Cravat** – Wide necktie tied at the front and tucked into the neck of a shirt or blouse.

**Crew** – Round close fitting neckline.

**Culotte** – Wide trousers resembling a skirt.

**Cummerbund** – Soft wide sash worn just above the waist.

# D

**Dart** – A tuck in the fabric, narrowing to a fine point, used to give shape usually over bust and thighs.

**Dolman** – Long Turkish robe worn open in front.

**Dolman sleeve** – Loose sleeve cut in one with the body of the coat.

**Dropped shoulder** – A shoulder line placed below the normal shoulder line.

# E

**Ease** – The distribution of fullness to fit, when one section of fabric is longer than its counterpart.

**Ease allowance** – The amount added to the body measurement when the pattern is designed, to allow for movement.

**Edge stitch** – To stitch close to the edge in order to hold the seam turnings exactly on the edge.

# F

**Facing** – The second section of fabric used to finish front edges and necklines.

**Faggoting** – An embroidery stitch to join two edges which do not quite meet.

**Flash baste** – Quick, diagonal tacking.

**Fly** – An opening which conceals a zip or buttons.

# G

**Gathering** – Drawing up fullness in fabric with a line of small running stitches, starting with a knot in the thread and easing the fabric along the thread from the other end.

**Godet** – A triangular section of fabric set into a seam for fullness or decoration, commonly in skirt seams at the hemline.

**Gusset** – A small piece of matching fabric, inserted to give ease, commonly at the underarm.

**Grain** – The lengthwise and crosswise direction of the yarn in a woven fabric. If these are not exactly at right angles to each other the fabric is said to be 'off grain'.

# H

**Harem pants** – Wide pants, gathered in at the ankle.

# I

**Interfacing** – A fusible fabric used to stiffen, stabilise and strengthen parts of garments such as collars, cuffs, front edges and waistbands.

**Interlining** – A third fabric used between a lining and outer fabric, usually for warmth.

# J

**Jabot** – Neck ruffle worn at the front of a blouse or shirt.

# L

**Lap** – To place one piece of fabric over another.

**Lapels** – The front part of a jacket that folds back to form the continuation of the collar.

**Layering** – To trim seam allowance edges so that one edge is slightly less than the other to make a finer, flatter edge when finished.

**Layout** – That part of the instruction sheet that shows how to place the fabric on the pattern.

# M

**Mandarin** – Small oriental-style standing collar.

**Marking** – Transferring the symbols on the paper pattern to the fabric by tailor's tacking or chalk.

**Mitre** – Diagonal seam line with fabric cut away to reduce bulk at a square corner.

**Mounting** – Using a second fabric to back another to give body and shape. It is cut using the same pattern pieces and the two fabrics are sewn as one (see Backing).

# N

**Nap** – The pile made by short fibres brushed in one direction e.g. on a fur or velvet fabric.

**Notches** – V-shaped outlines in the cut edge of a seam allowance signifying which edges should be joined together and where.

**Notions** – Haberdashery items such as threads, buttons etc. needed to complete garment.

# O

**Overblouse** – Blouse intended to be worn outside skirt or trousers and not tucked in at waist.

**Oversized** – Large, very loose fitting top or shirt with a great deal of designer ease.

# P

**Peplum** – Short flounce over the hips attached to a jacket or blouse at the waist.

**Petersham** – A thick, corded ribbon. Curved petersham is used to finish the waist of a skirt either as a substitute for a waistband or to stiffen a fabric waistband.

**Pre-shrunk fabric** – Fabric that has been treated, usually with steam, to shrink it before it is made up to avoid further shrinkage.

**Princess line** – Shaping achieved with long fitted seam lines without darts.

# R

**Raw edge** – an unfinished edge of fabric which may fray.

**Reinforce** – To strengthen fabric where it is subject to strain such as the corner of a welt pocket or buttonholes. It is achieved by extra stitching or backing the area with iron-on interfacing.

# S

**Seam allowance** – The amount of fabric allowed for turnings when stitching pieces together – 1.5 cm ($\frac{5}{8}$ in) unless otherwise indicated in the pattern.

**Seamline** – The line indicated for the stitching.

**Selvedge** – The finished edge of a woven fabric.

**Shank** – The stem of the button which allows for the thickness of the fabric. If the button has no shank it is formed with thread.

**Shirring** – gathering up fabric with several rows of elasticated thread.

**Shirtwaister** – A dress with fashion detail similar to a shirt.

**Slash** – A long straight cut in a fabric indicated on the pattern, such as a faced cuff opening.

**Snip** – A short cut in the fabric.

**Stay** – A tape used to stabilise a line of stitching.

# T

**Tailoring** – Constructing a garment to a high standard with special hand sewing and pressing techniques.

**Taper** – Stitching at a slight diagonal line, becoming gradually smaller at one end.

**Tension** – The degree of tightness in the line of machine stitching.

**Toile** – A pattern of a garment made up in a cheap cloth, such as muslin, before the final design, usually for fitting purposes or to make copies.

**Top-stitching** – Bold machine stitching parallel to the seam or edge, worked from the right side.

**Tuck** – A fold in the fabric held in place with stitching.

**Tunic** – A long top, usually of fairly straight cut, to be worn over another garment.

**Turtleneck** – High, turned over, close-fitting neckline.

# U

**Underlay** – A strip of fabric placed underneath the main fabric to give support, such as a pleat underlay.

# V

**Vent** – A lapped opening as in the back of a tailored jacket.

# W

**Warp** – The lengthwise threads, those that are set up vertically when a fabric is woven.

**Weft** – The threads that run across the warp when the fabric is woven.

**Welt** – A strip of fabric stitched to an edge – as in a welt pocket.

# Y

**Yoke** – Fitted part of garment, e.g. across the shoulders of a shirt, designed to allow the rest of the garment to hang from it.

# PATTERN ESSENTIALS

There are a few basic pieces of information that you'll need to make up your pattern. They briefly describe some terms and the meaning of symbols used on the pattern and make-up sheet.

Below is the style guide which should be useful when you need a quick reference.

## FIRST PREPARE YOUR PATTERN

Select the pattern pieces according to the view you are making.

This pattern is made to body measurements with ease allowed for comfort and style. If your body measurements differ from those on the pattern envelope adjust the pieces before placing them on the fabric.

Check your nape to waist and dress length; if necessary, alter the pattern. Lengthening and shortening lines are indicated.

**To Lengthen:**
Cut pattern between printed lines and place paper underneath. Spread pattern the required amount and pin to paper.

**To Shorten:**
Fold at the printed lines to form a pleat half the amount to be shortened, i.e. 1.3 cm ($\frac{1}{2}$") deep to shorten 2.5 cm (1").

## STUDY YOUR PATTERN MARKINGS

▶ STRAIGHT GRAIN ◀——————▶
Place an even distance from selvedge or a straight thread.

▶ FOLD ▼ ▼
Place on fold of fabric.

▶ LENGTHENING AND SHORTENING LINES ═══
 
▶ SEAM ALLOWANCE ⌐1.5cm⌐
1.5 cm ($\frac{5}{8}$") unless otherwise stated.

▶ NOTCHES ◇
Match corresponding notches.

▶ CUTTING LINES ─ ∙ ─ ∙ ─
Multi patterns have different cutting lines for different sizes. See the key on the printed pattern.

## CUTTING DIRECTIONS

For double thickness fabric, fold fabric with right side inside and place pattern on wrong side of fabric. For single fabric, place pattern on right side of fabric.

Please note that pattern pieces may interlock more closely when cutting smaller sizes.

Cut notches out from cutting line. After cutting out and BEFORE removing pattern from fabric, transfer all pattern markings to fabric using Tailor Tacks or Tailor's chalk.

## TAILOR TACKS

With double thread make two loose stitches forming loop through fabric layers and pattern leaving long ends. Cut loop to remove pattern. Snip thread between fabric layers. Leave tufts.

# CUTTING LAYOUTS

▨ Shaded area denotes fabric.

▢ Pattern pieces placed printed side up.

⬚ Pattern pieces cut a second time.

✳ Pattern pieces placed printed side down.

## ▶ FABRIC KEY FOR ILLUSTRATIONS

Right side    Wrong side    Interfacing    Lining

1.5 cm ($\frac{5}{8}$") SEAM ALLOWANCE IS GIVEN UNLESS OTHERWISE STATED.

Press all seams open unless otherwise stated. Snip if necessary to press seams flat.

Pin or tack seams, WITH RIGHT SIDES TOGETHER, matching notches and circles accurately. Fit garments before stitching.

## ▶ MACHINE NEATENING

Machine zigzag over raw edges of seams, hems and facings.

## ▶ INTERFACING

*Iron-on,* place on wrong side of fabric and fuse in place following manufacturer's instructions. *Sew-in,* tack to wrong side of fabric 1.3 cm ($\frac{1}{2}$") from raw edges. Trim to tacking.

## ▶ LAYERING

Trim seam allowance in layers and interfacing close to stitching.

Layer enclosed seams.   Trim corners.   Snip inner curves.   Notch outer curves.

## ▶ STAY STITCH

Stitch 3 mm ($\frac{1}{8}$") from seam line in seam allowance. (Usually 1.3 cm ($\frac{1}{2}$") from raw edges.)

## ▶ UNDERSTITCH

Press facing away from garment, onto seam allowance. Facing uppermost, stitch close to seam through facing and seam allowance.

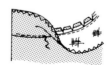

## ▶ EDGE-STITCH

Right side uppermost, stitch close to seam or finished edge.

## ▶ TOP-STITCH

Stitch 6 mm ($\frac{1}{4}$") to 1 cm ($\frac{3}{8}$") from edge-stitching, using presser foot as a guide.

# INDEX

Page numbers in *italic* refer to the illustrations